STE[
Test Prep

LAW ESSENTIALS

Business Associations

Governing Law

3rd edition

3 2 1

ISBN-13: 978-1-9547252-4-9

Sterling Test Prep products are available at quantity discounts.

For more information, contact info@sterling–prep.com.

Sterling Test Prep
6 Liberty Square #11
Boston, MA 02109

©2022 Sterling Test Prep
Published by Sterling Test Prep
Printed in the U.S.A.

Customer Satisfaction Guarantee

Your feedback is important because we strive to provide the highest quality prep materials. Email us comments or suggestions.

info@sterling–prep.com

We reply to emails – check your spam folder

Thank you for choosing our book!

STERLING
Test Prep

Thousands of students use our study aids to prepare for law school exams and to pass the bar!

Passing the bar is essential for admission to practice law and launching your legal career.

This preparation guide describes the principles of substantive law governing the correct answers to exam questions. It was developed by legal professionals and law instructors who possess extensive credentials and have been admitted to practice law in several jurisdictions. The content is clearly presented and systematically organized for targeted preparation.

The performance on individual questions has been correlated with success or failure on the bar. By analyzing previously administered exams, the authors identified these predictive items and assembled the rules of law that govern the answers to questions tested. Learn the essential governing law to make fine-line distinctions among related principles and decide between tough choices on the exam. This knowledge is vital to excel in law school finals and pass the bar exam.

We look forward to being an essential part of your preparation and wish you great success in the legal profession!

210713vgr

Law Essentials series

Constitutional Law	Criminal Law and Criminal Procedure
Contracts	Business Associations
Evidence	Conflict of Laws
Real Property	Family Law
Torts	Secured Transactions
Civil Procedure	Trusts and Estates

Visit our Amazon store

Comprehensive Glossary of Legal Terms

Over 2,100 essential legal terms defined and explained. An excellent reference source for law students, practitioners and readers seeking an understanding of legal vocabulary and its application.

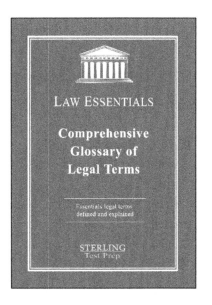

Landmark U.S. Supreme Court Cases: Essential Summaries

Learn important constitutional cases that shaped American law. Understand how the evolving needs of society intersect with the U.S. Constitution. Short summaries of seminal Supreme Court cases focused on issues and holdings.

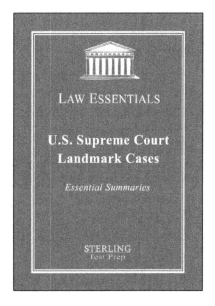

Visit our Amazon store

Table of Contents

BUSINESS ASSOCIATIONS GOVERNING LAW (*continued*)

BUSINESS ASSOCIATIONS GOVERNING LAW (*continued*)

BUSINESS ASSOCIATIONS GOVERNING LAW (*continued*)

BUSINESS ASSOCIATIONS GOVERNING LAW (*continued*)

EXAM INFORMATION, PREP & TEST-TAKING STRATEGIES (*continued*)

EXAM INFORMATION, PREP & TEST-TAKING STRATEGIES (*continued*)

APPENDIX (*continued*)

Business Associations
Governing Law

The subject matter outline for Business Associations is divided into four sections: Agency, Partnerships, Corporations, and Limited Liability Companies. The exam often tests either Corporations and LLCs or agencies and partnerships, though occasionally it includes both. Maximize your score by mastering the governing law on these highly tested topics.

For Agency and Partnerships, the principles of the Uniform Partnership Act (UPA), the Revised Uniform Partnership Act (RUPA), or the Restatement (Second) of Agency are generally applied. The commonly tested Agency issues include actual authority, apparent authority, vicarious and direct liability, and principal and agent liability for contracts entered into by the agent. For Partnership, frequently tested items are formation, fiduciary duties, Limited Liability Partnerships (LLPs), Limited Partnerships (LPs), creditors rights, dissolution, and termination.

For Corporations, the principles of the Model Business Corporation Act (MBCA) and the Revised Model Business Corporation Act (RMBCA) apply. The commonly tested Corporations items include fiduciary duties and shareholder (i.e., derivative) lawsuits. LLCs may be tested instead of Corporations. The frequent LLC questions pertain to piercing the LLC veil and fiduciary duties. Many of the same principles apply to partnerships, corporations, and LLCs.

STERLING
Test Prep

Agency: Relationships

Agency

An agency relationship occurs when one person (the agent or servant) acts on behalf of another (the principal or master).

The legal ramifications that occur because of these acts are delineated in the law of agency.

The five types of agents are general agent, special agent, subagent, agency coupled with an interest, and servant (or employee).

Establishing agency

Agency relationships are generally formed by the mutual consent of a principal and an agent, although not always. An agency can arise as an express agency, implied agency, apparent agency, and agency by ratification. The most common form of agency is express agency. In an express agency, the agent has the authority to contract or otherwise act on the principal's behalf as expressly stated in the agency agreement. Additionally, the agent may possess certain implied or apparent authority to act on the principal's behalf.

Express agency occurs when a principal and an agent expressly agree to enter into an agency agreement with each other. Express agency contracts can be oral or written unless the Statute of Frauds stipulates that they must be written. A power of attorney is an example of an express agency. An implied agency is an agency that occurs from the parties' conduct rather than from a prior agreement between them. The facts determine the extent of the agent's authority.

Implied authority can be conferred by *industry custom*, *prior dealing between the parties*, the agent's position, and acts deemed necessary to carry out the agent's duties.

Apparent agency (or *agency by estoppel*) arises when a principal creates the appearance of an agency that does not exist. Where an apparent agency is established, the principal is estopped from denying the agency relationship and is bound to contracts entered into by the apparent agent while acting within the scope of the apparent agency. The principal's actions (not the agent's) create an apparent agency.

An *agency by ratification* occurs when a person misrepresents themself as another's agent when they are not, and the purported principal ratifies (accepts) the unauthorized act. In such cases, the principal is bound to perform, and the agent is relieved of liability for misrepresentation.

Creation formalities – capacity

An agency relationship is consensual.

An agency relationship can be created without a writing showing an agreement to create an agency relationship.

A minor may act as an agent, even lacking the capacity to contract.

A principal must have the capacity to enter into contractual transactions before they can employ an agent to do the same on their behalf.

Proof of agency

To prove an agency relationship, the party with the burden of proof must show the principal and agent's intent to enter the relationship.

An agency relationship does not automatically arise because of a kinship relationship between the purported agent and principal.

For example, a person who owns the property as a co-tenant is not automatically the other co-tenant's agent.

The person desiring to establish an agency relationship can introduce the alleged agent's testimony from which an agency may be found.

The alleged agent cannot testify to the conclusion that they entered a principal agency relationship.

Presumption of agency

In actions arising out of a motor vehicle accident, evidence that an automobile was registered in the defendant's name *is prima facie* evidence that it was being operated by a person whose conduct the defendant is legally responsible for.

The defendant may prove the absence of such responsibility.

Such proof of legal responsibility is the basis for using the insurance policy covering the motor vehicle to satisfy tort claims arising out of the accident.

Termination of agency for at-will of parties

An agency relationship is terminable at will by the principal or agent except when it is coupled with an interest.

An agency is coupled with an interest if the agent has legal rights in the agency's subject matter.

For example, a liability insurer has the right to defend the insured because of its interest in the litigation

Even though the relationship is terminable, a contract creating the agency has an effect beyond the termination. If the termination constitutes a breach of contract, the non-breaching party can sue for damages but cannot sue to enforce the contract specifically.

Termination by operation of law

Except for agency relationships created by a law authorizing durable powers of attorney and except when an agency is coupled with an interest, an agency is terminated by the principal's death, insanity, or bankruptcy.

Durable powers and powers coupled with an interest are not terminated by the principal's death, insanity, or bankruptcy.

Notice of termination of agency

Notice must be given to persons who dealt with the principal through the agent when an agency relationship is terminated.

If notice is not given, the principal may be held liable on subsequent contracts on the theory of apparent authority of the agent.

Where persons have not dealt with the agent, notice by publication is sufficient.

Notice is not required when the agency is terminated by death, insanity, or bankruptcy of the principal.

Notes for active learning

Agency: Vicarious Liability of Principal for Acts of Agent

Tort liability

The law of agency imposes liability for tortuous acts the agent (servant) commits upon the principal (master).

The first step in imposing vicarious liability for another's torts is to determine if a principal–agent relationship existed.

Right to control

The *right to control* the tortfeasor (agent) acts is the critical element determining if a master–servant (principal–agent) relationship exists.

If the tortfeasor has the right to control performance and only general goals are specified, the tortfeasor is more likely to be classified as an independent contractor.

Although no test is conclusive in determining if the purported master has the right to control:

1) details of the work assignment (direct boss *vs*. general job description), factors such as:

   (a) the method of payment (hourly wage *vs*. fee for entire job), and

   (b) length of employment (short term is consistent with independent contractor relationship),

2) distinct business (favors independent contractor relationship),

3) degree of supervision (the greater the supervision, the more likely that the relationship will be classified as employer-employee),

4) skills of the actual tortfeasor; the higher the skill level, the more the relationship is deemed an independent contractor).

An *employer can* be *vicariously liable* for an employee's negligence but *will not* be *liable* for intentionally wrongful or criminal acts (e.g., assault, murder) unless the employee's intentionally wrongful acts were *required* by the employment or *foreseeable*.

Case law classified the following special agent-principal relationships.

Borrowed servants

A person who borrows the services of a tortfeasor and controls their activity will be vicariously liable for torts while the servant is on loan to the master.

Temporary servants

A person may be a servant for the commission of a single act, and vicarious liability will be imposed upon the person who has a temporary master's role.

Sub-servants

If an employee in an employer–employee relationship employs a sub-servant to perform tasks usually assigned to the employee, the employee is only liable for the torts of a subservient committed while engaged in work performed with express or implied authority.

Master–servant relationship: *respondeat superior*

Respondeat superior is Latin for "let the master answer."

Vicarious liability is imposed upon a master for the negligent torts of their servant committed while performing on the master's business and acting within the scope of their authority.

The acts of a servant pursuing their personal business when the tort occurred will not be imputed to the master.

Nor will the master be vicariously liable in tort if the servant has substantially deviated from an authorized route.

Use of force by the servant

If the servant commits an intentional tort (e.g., assault and battery) in doing the master's work, the master will be held vicariously liable.

If an employee of a public carrier injures a customer through misconduct while engaged in the performance of a contract of carriage, the company is vicariously liable.

Independent contractors

A person who uses due care in hiring an independent contractor is not liable for negligence, except when the independent contractor is engaged in:

> 1) inherently dangerous activities (e.g., blasting);
>
> 2) creates a nuisance;
>
> 3) where the premises worked on are in dangerous disrepair; and
>
> 4) where a nondelegable duty is imposed upon the person hiring the independent contractor.

Principal–agent tort liability

A principal is liable for nonphysical torts such as deceit, defamation, and interference with contractual or advantageous relations if the act was expressly, impliedly, or apparently authorized.

Procedural Considerations

The master and servant are not joint tortfeasors.

A master is entitled to indemnification from their servant if the basis of liability is *respondeat superior*.

Notes for active learning

Agency: Contract Liability

A disclosed agent, acting within the scope of their authority, which enters a contract creates a contract between the principal and the other contracting party.

The agent is not liable on that contract.

Actual authority

The most crucial form of authority which will cause an agent to bind a principal is actual authority.

Such authority may be expressed, implied by a course of dealings, or incidental as necessary to accomplish an act expressly authorized.

When the principal is unavailable, an agent is impliedly authorized to take reasonable measures in an emergency.

Apparent authority

If a person has by acts or words indicated to a third party that a particular individual has the authority to act, they will be liable for contracts made on their behalf by the purported agent even if there is no actual authority if the third party reasonably relies to their detriment on the purported principal's representations.

General and special agents

A *general agent* is employed to transact the principal's business and has the authority to conduct that type of business without a specific grant of authority for each transaction.

A *special agent* is employed for a specific transaction and cannot bind the principal beyond the specific authority conferred.

A party who has the authority to complete a transaction has the implied authority to perform the acts incidental to their primary mission.

Secret limitations on such incidental powers do not provide a defense to a principal on the issue of authority unless the third party dealing with the agent becomes aware of them before making the contract.

Imputed knowledge

If an issue in litigation is whether the principal had knowledge and whether that knowledge was imparted (or notice given) to the agent, knowledge (or notice) is imputed to the principal even if the agent does not communicate what was learned while representing the principal.

Ratification

Ratification is an additional process to hold a principal liable for contracts made by an agent without authority.

Words, conduct, or silence may prove ratification.

If a principal ratifies an unauthorized agent's act, they must ratify all conduct and accept burdens and benefits.

Valid ratification occurs only when the following conditions are met:

> 1) the principal must have knowledge of material facts regarding the transaction;
>
> 2) the agent must have intended to represent the principal at the time of the unauthorized act; and
>
> 3) the ratifying party must have been in existence at the time of the act.

A corporation cannot ratify pre-incorporation contracts.

Valid ratification is retroactive to the time that the purported agent acted.

Once ratified, the contract is irrevocable unless voidable for fraud, duress, illegality, or lack of capacity.

Agency: Fiduciary Duties Between Principal and Agent

Fiduciary duties

The agent owes the principal duties in two categories:

> fiduciary duties (care and loyalty), and

> a set of general duties imposed by agency law.

These general duties are not unique to agency law; they are duties owed by an employee to the employer.

The *agent's duties* include:

> 1) to act on behalf of and be subject to the control of the principal,

> 2) act within the scope of authority or power delegated by the principal,

> 3) discharge duties with appropriate care and diligence,

> 4) avoid conflict between their interests and those of the principal, and

> 5) promptly tender to the principal monies collected on the principal's behalf.

The *principal's duties* include:

> 1) to compensate the agent as agreed, and

> 2) indemnify the agent against claims, liabilities, and expenses incurred in discharging duties assigned by the principal.

Rights and liabilities between agent and principal

A fiduciary *duty of care* is imposed on the agent to avoid acts or omissions, which could be reasonably foreseen to injure or harm other people.

The agent owes a fiduciary *duty of loyalty* to the principal, which stands for the principle that corporate directors and officers make decisions in their capacities as fiduciaries and act without personal economic conflict.

The *duty of obedience* means that the agent must obey reasonable directions concerning the manner of performance.

The agent can be sued for breach of these duties.

An agent is required to act in the manner specified by the agreement creating the agency.

If the agent acts contrary, they can be sued for breach of the agency contract.

The principal is typically required to pay compensation to the agent for services, either the amount in the agency contract or the services' fair value if no amount was agreed.

If a person has acted as a double agent for parties with conflicting interests without informing both, they are barred from recovering compensation from either.

An agent is entitled to indemnification for expenses and liabilities incurred in the performance of their duties.

If held liable on a contract they negotiated as an agent for an undisclosed principal, and the agent and principal are each liable on such contracts, the agent is entitled to indemnification from liability by the principal.

Agent, principal and third-party rights and liabilities

If an agent is disclosed and makes a contract within the scope of their authority, the agent is not personally liable on the contract.

If the principal is undisclosed, the third party may elect to sue the agent instead of the principal.

To bar the third party from suing the person not sued when the election was made, the election to sue the agent or the principal must be made with knowledge that the agent acted for the undisclosed principal.

The principal is not liable for the payment of a judgment obtained against the agent.

If the contract is in the form of a negotiable instrument, only the agent who is the signatory to that instrument can be sued.

An agent may be liable to the third party in a deceit action, but not on the contract, nor any breach of warranty of authority theory if the agent enters into a contract on behalf of a disclosed principal beyond the agent's scope of authority.

The third party is not able to prevail against the principal.

The agent may be held liable to the principal for breach of fiduciary duty or contract if a principal is held liable in the contract because the conduct of the agent acted beyond the express authority granted.

Partnerships: Creation of Partnerships

Formation of a partnership

A partnership is a business entity created when two or more people associate to carry on a business and do not choose another form of business entity (e.g., corporation, limited liability company).

The key test of whether a partnership has been formed is the parties' intent to join efforts to undertake some business enterprise.

No formal documents are required to form the partnership.

No written partnership agreement is required, nor must there be an oral agreement.

The conduct of the parties can form a partnership with a set of common law attributes.

The capacity needed to enter a partnership is the same as the capacity to contract.

An appropriate answer to many business entity questions includes an analysis of whether the conduct of the parties is sufficient to warrant a finding that a partnership has been created.

The factors of whether a partnership has been formed are:

1) Did the parties agree to share the profits of an enterprise?

   A countervailing analysis is that payment to one of the parties is a loan, repayment of a debt, or payment for services rendered rather than a share of the profits.

2) Are the parties sharing gross returns?

3) Do the parties own property jointly?

   A countervailing analysis is that ownership of property by itself does not cause the co-owners to be partners.

   Partnership requires participation in the management of the business.

Partnership by estoppel

A person can incur partnership liability by holding themself out to be a partner or permit someone to represent to others that they are a partner even without a partnership relationship.

> That conduct renders liability for the debts of the partnership to a creditor who has relied on those representations.

> If those representations were made privately, only recipients of the representations could sue.

> If made publicly, liability extends to anyone who has knowledge of the representations and relied upon them.

A person held out as a partner is an agent of those consenting to the representation and can bind them as if a partner.

For example, placing a lawyer's name on letterhead with other lawyers can constitute a holding out that the other persons on the letterhead are partners.

Partnerships: Power and Liability of Partners

Fiduciary relationship among partners

Each partner owes other partners a *fiduciary duty of loyalty* and the utmost *good faith*.

Unless partners agree, a partner must not compete with the partnership within its business scope or take a business opportunity that could be performed by the partnership for its benefit.

A partner must account to the partnership for their profits, or a court could impose a constructive trust to hold the business opportunity for the benefit of the partnership.

Partners must disclose material facts relating to the partnership business to other partners.

If a partner uses partnership property for their private gain, they must account for the profits of the partnership.

Partner's right to an accounting

A partner is entitled to a formal accounting to determine the partnership's profits and losses and each partner's share:

1) if partners wrongfully exclude them from the partnership business;

2) if the partnership agreement provides for an accounting;

3) when another partner has breached their fiduciary duty to the partnership;

4) whenever it is just and reasonable, each must be given an accounting.

Each partner is entitled to access the partnership books, which must be kept at the partnership's principal place of business.

Rights and duties of partners

If no partnership agreement provides otherwise, each partner is entitled to an equal share of the partnership profits.

If a partnership is being liquidated, each partner is entitled to be repaid their capital contribution after partnership debts have been satisfied.

After capital contributions have been repaid, each partner is entitled to their share of partnership profits.

Those shares will be equal among the partners unless the partnership agreement provides differently.

If there are partnership losses, they will be shared equally by the partners unless the agreement provides a different arrangement.

Ordinarily, if one partner is entitled to more than a pro-rata share of profits, they will be required to pay the same share of the losses.

A partner has a right to be reimbursed by the partnership for payments made and liabilities reasonably incurred in the ordinary and proper conduct of the partnership business or for expenditures made to protect and preserve partnership property.

Unless the partnership agreement provides otherwise, a partner is not entitled to interest on their capital account.

A partner who makes a payment or advances beyond the amount they agreed to contribute is entitled to interest from the date of the payment or advance for that additional amount.

A partner is not ordinarily entitled to a salary for services rendered to the partnership, absent an agreement.

A surviving partner is entitled to reasonable compensation for winding up the partnership.

Unless the partnership agreement provides otherwise, each partner has an equal right in business management and conduct.

Ordinarily, a vote of the majority of the partners is necessary to decide any matter.

No act in contravention of an agreement may be done without the partners' consent.

No person can become a partner in an existing partnership unless existing partners consent.

Partners cannot sue each other for damages in an action at law for partnership matters.

The proper remedy is an equitable lawsuit for an accounting.

Partnerships: Partnership Property and Property Rights

Partnership property

When funds of a partnership are used to acquire property, the property is "partnership property" even if title to the property is taken in the name of an individual partner.

Each partner is a co-owner with partners of partnership property, holding as tenants-in-partnership.

A partner has the right to use partnership property for partnership purposes but cannot use it other than for partnership purposes without the consent of the partnership.

A partner cannot assign their interest in partnership property unless the partners consent.

A partner's interest in partnership property cannot be attached or sold pursuant to execution unless the attachment is based on a claim against the partnership.

Upon death, partnership property vests in the surviving partners and is not an asset of the partner's estate.

The claim of the estate against the partnership is for an accounting.

The partnership interest

A partner's interest consists of their share of the profits and surplus of the partnership.

Unlike specific partnership property, a partner's interest is assignable.

The assignment of a partnership interest by a partner does not dissolve the partnership.

The assignee has rights in the asset assigned (i.e., profits and surplus).

The assignee is not a partner and has no partnership rights.

The assignee is only entitled to receive the profits due to the assignor.

If the partnership is dissolved, the assignee receives the assignor's interest.

A judgment creditor cannot sell the partnership interest to satisfy a claim until the other partners have the opportunity to redeem the partner's interest in the partnership.

Management of the partnership

A partner has the right to manage the partnership where matters are decided in the absence of an agreement by a majority vote of partners.

No person can become a partner without the unanimous consent of the partners.

Conveyance of real property

A partner who has been authorized by the partnership can convey real property owned by the partnership by executing a deed in proper form.

Partnerships: Relationship of Partners to Third Parties

Agency

The act of a partner within the scope of the partnership binds the partnership, except when the partner lacks authority to perform the act, and the third party knows of that lack of authority.

A statement by a partner acting within their authority is admissible as an admission in evidence against the partnership.

There are specific limitations on a partner's authority unless granted by the partners.

The *specific limitations on the authority* of any partner are:

1) assign partnership property in trust for creditors or on the assignee's promise to pay the partnership's debts;

2) dispose of the business's goodwill;

3) do anything which would make it impossible to carry on its ordinary business;

4) confess a judgment;

5) submit a partnership claim or liability to arbitration or reference.

Notice to partner as notice to the partnership

A notice given to one partner or knowledge acquired by one partner on a matter related to partnership affairs is imputed to the partnership unless fraud is committed on the partnership by or with that partner's consent.

Liability of partners for general partnerships

In a general partnership, as opposed to a limited liability partnership, partners are jointly liable for the partnership's liabilities to the extent of their personal and partnership assets.

When a partnership as an entity is sued, at least one partner must be named a defendant.

Because a general partnership obligation is joint, each partner is individually liable for the entire amount of the obligation.

If a partner pays a partnership debt, they are entitled to be reimbursed from the partnership if there are partnership assets available for reimbursement.

If a partner pays more than their pro-rata share of a partnership debt and cannot recover from the partnership, they are entitled to recover from their co-partners the amount which they paid above their partnership share.

A dormant partner (i.e., partner not active in partnership affairs) is liable for partnership obligations in a general partnership.

A person who joins a partnership already in existence is liable for partnership obligations arising before joining the partnership only to the extent of their investment in the partnership.

Liability of partners for Limited Partnerships (LP)

In a limited partnership, a limited partner who has no voice in the partnership management is liable on partnership debts and obligations only to the extent of their interest in the partnership.

General partners are jointly liable for partnership obligations, and their assets can be reached to satisfy the partnership debt.

Liability of partners for Limited Liability Partnerships (LLP)

Common law partnerships can become Limited Liability Partnerships by registering as Limited Liability Partnerships.

When a partnership becomes a Limited Liability Partnership, the partnership property remains liable to satisfy partnership obligations.

Joint and several liability is assessed against the partners only for partners' wrongful acts according to the partnership and money misapplied by the partnership.

A partner in a registered Limited Liability Partnership is not personally liable directly or indirectly for debts, obligations, and liabilities of the partnership except for matters arising in whole or in part from the partner's negligence, wrongful acts, errors, or omissions.

A partner must carry a designated amount of liability insurance prescribed by that profession's regulatory body to benefit from a Limited Liability Partnership rendering professional services.

The limited liability partnership's name must end with the designation *Registered Limited Liability Partnership* or *Limited Liability Partnership* or their abbreviation LLP.

Most general partnerships are now Limited Liability Partnerships.

Partnerships: Dissolution

Causes of dissolution of partnerships

A common law partnership is dissolved within the terms of the partnership agreement by:

1) termination of the term or undertaking;

2) the action of a partner, including death or bankruptcy in a partnership at will;

3) agreement of the partners; or

4) expulsion of a partner.

Winding up is a process whereby all company assets are realized and used to pay off the liabilities and members.

A partnership is terminated when all partnership affairs are wound up.

Dissolution puts an end to the life of the partnership after winding up.

Any partner may dissolve the partnership in contravention of the partnership agreement, and the partner who wrongfully causes a dissolution is liable for damages to any partner injured.

When a partnership is wrongfully dissolved, the remaining partners can continue the business.

Any partner may sue for dissolution on the grounds of a partner's:

1) insanity or incapacity;

2) conduct prejudicial to business; or

3) willful breach of the agreement or conduct rendering the business impracticable.

A dissolution decree is available if the partnership's business can only be carried on at a loss or if other circumstances render a dissolution equitable.

Effect of dissolution on partner's authority

In the process of dissolution, a partner only has the authority to bind the other partners concerning winding up partnership affairs and completing unfinished transactions.

Under agency principles, the partnership is bound on new obligations after dissolution incurred by a partner acting under the following circumstances.

If a partner does business within the apparent scope of the partnership business with a third party who had extended credit before dissolution, the partnership is liable if the third party did not know of the dissolution and the notice of dissolution has not been properly published.

Winding up the partnership

All partners who have not engaged in the partnership's wrongful dissolution have an equal right to wind up the partnership.

Partners may delegate exclusive power to one or more partners.

A partner who engages in winding up the partnership must pay debts, complete unfinished contracts and transactions, collect debts, dispose of partnership property, and close the business.

Continuance of partnership after dissolution

If wrongfully dissolved, the remaining partners can continue the partnership.

The partners must settle the dissolving partner's claims but can deduct damages for breach.

If they continue the business, the continuing partners must indemnify the dissolving partner against partnership liabilities.

Partners may continue the partnership's business when a partner is expelled, retires, dies (if they or their representative consents), or the partnership agreement provides continuation.

If the retiring partner or deceased partner's estate does not settle with the continuing partners, they have the option of receiving either the value of the dissolution shares plus interest or in place of interest, the profits attributable to the use of their right in the firm property from the time of dissolution to settlement.

When the partners continue the partnership business, the original partnership's creditors become creditors of the continuing partnership.

Distribution of partnership assets

If the business is not continued, the partners must wind it up by liquidating its assets if necessary, settling its obligations, and distributing the remaining assets to the partners.

Assets include partnership property and, if necessary, any partners' contributions needed to pay obligations to creditors.

Assets are distributed in the following order of priority:

> 1) debts to non-partner creditors;
>
> 2) debts to partner creditors;
>
> 3) return of capital contributions of partners;
>
> 4) payment of profits to partners.

Partnerships: Limited Partnerships

Formation of Limited Partnerships

A limited partnership (LP) can carry on any business that a general partnership can and is formed by filing with the Secretary of State a signed certificate, detailing the incidents and composition of the business, the name, including the words limited partnership, and the names and business addresses of the general partners.

A limited partnership is composed of:

1) one or more general partners, who manage the business and are personally liable without limitation for partnership obligations; and

2) one or more limited partners contributing capital and sharing in profits but have no control or management of the business; limited partners' liability is limited to their contribution.

Profits and losses of a limited partnership and distributions of assets are allocated following the written partnership agreement.

If the agreement is silent, profits and losses are distributed based on a partner's contribution.

Obligations of limited partners

A limited partner is obligated to the partnership to perform the promise they made to obtain the limited partnership interest.

Rights and powers of limited partners

A limited partner has the right to inspect and copy the required partnership records and tax returns, obtain from the general partners and full information about the financial condition and state of the business, and such other information as is just and reasonable.

The partnership agreement may grant voting powers to all or some limited partners upon any matter.

General partners

A general partner in a limited partnership is the equivalent of a general partner in a general partnership.

Assignment of Limited Partnership interests

A limited partnership interest is generally assignable.

While an assignee is entitled only to receive the distributions to which the assignor would have been entitled, an assignee may become a limited partner if:

> 1) the assignor gives rights per authority granted in the partnership agreement, or

> 2) absent such authority, all partners consent.

Distributions of Limited Partnership interests

A partner is entitled to receive interim distributions following the terms of the partnership agreement.

Upon withdrawal, the withdrawing partner can receive distribution to which they are entitled under the agreement or, absent such provision, the fair value of their partnership interest.

Dissolution of Limited Partnership interests

A limited partnership is dissolved at the time or upon the events specified in writing in the partnership agreement or upon all partners' written consent.

A court may decree dissolution on application by a partner whenever it is not reasonably practicable to carry on the business in conformity with the partnership agreement.

Business Trusts

Business trusts as unincorporated associations

A business trust is an unincorporated business association created by a trust instrument, which transfers the business property to trustees who hold and manage it to benefit the trust certificate holders.

The trust provides limited liability for the beneficiaries unless they retain too much control.

The beneficiaries can neither elect nor remove the trustees.

If the trust instrument vests such control in the beneficiaries that the trustees are merely their agents, the trust will be deemed a partnership, and beneficiaries will be personally liable.

Factors indicating *too much control* of the business trust include:

> the power to elect trustees,
>
> to remove trustees and fill vacancies,
>
> to instruct trustees,
>
> to amend the trust, or
>
> terminate the trust.

Beneficiaries may petition the court to remove a trustee for violating their fiduciary duty.

A majority vote of the trustees binds the trust.

Trustees are personally liable on contracts unless the contract provides otherwise.

However, if the trustee has not exceeded their authority, they are entitled to reimbursement from trust assets.

An unsatisfied creditor may reach and apply trust property by being substituted for the trustee to the extent of indemnification right.

Notes for active learning

Corporations: Nature of Corporate Existence

The corporation as a separate entity

A corporation is created by filing appropriate incorporation documents with the Secretary of State and paying the appropriate fee.

A corporation is a legal entity separate and distinct from its owners, the shareholders.

Its owners are not ordinarily personally liable for its liabilities.

The status of the corporation in the constitution

A corporation has constitutional protection *as a person* under:

> Fifth and Fourteenth Amendment due process clauses,
>
> Equal protection clause of the Fourteenth Amendment, and
>
> Fourth Amendment search and seizure clause.

It is *not a person* under:

> Fifth Amendment clause against self-incrimination, and,
>
> Privileges and Immunities clause of Article IV § 2.

Subordination of shareholder debt

If an inadequately capitalized corporation becomes insolvent and shareholders hold substantial corporate debt, a court can subordinate the shareholder's debt to other unsecured debt paid before the shareholders.

For an inadequately capitalized corporation, shareholders lose payment priority on their debt.

Shareholders are not personally liable for the corporation's debt.

Notes for active learning

Corporations: Organizing the Corporation

Duties and liabilities of promoters during pre-incorporation

Before incorporation papers are filed, persons joining to form the corporation are *promoters*.

The promoters' relationship is a joint venture or partnership whereby each owes the other a fiduciary duty of *full disclosure* and *fair dealing*.

Promoters are agents of each other, having the power to bind promoters to contracts made by one.

Until they form the corporation, they are personally liable for obligations incurred.

Once the promoters file the corporation papers (i.e., articles of incorporation) and have the status of incorporators, but before the corporation issues shares, the incorporators may exercise the powers of shareholders.

The organizational meeting

One or more persons at least eighteen years of age may act as incorporators.

A corporation may act as an incorporator.

At the organizational meeting, the incorporators adopt by-laws, elect directors and officers, and prepare and sign the articles of incorporation (*articles of organization* for an LLC).

The *articles of incorporation* and the filing fee are tendered to the Secretary of State to create a corporation.

The articles of incorporation

The *articles of incorporation* (articles of organization for an LLC) are the highest source of authority in the corporation's internal documents.

In the event of a conflict with the by-laws or directors' actions, the provisions in the articles of incorporation prevail.

The articles of incorporation must contain:

1) name of the corporation (or include Inc., Incorporated, or words which indicate the entity as a corporation);

2) number of shares the corporation is authorized to issue and required description of additional classes or series of shares;

3) names and addresses of the incorporators who form a corporation.

The articles of incorporation may contain provisions concerning:

  1) the purposes for which the corporation was organized,

  2) managing the business and regulating the corporation's affairs, defining, limiting, and regulating powers of the corporation, board of directors, and shareholders.

The articles of incorporation contain provisions that must be included to be effective.

The articles of incorporation may contain exculpatory provisions concerning directors, but they cannot eliminate the liability of a director for:

  1) breach of the *duty of loyalty* to the corporations or its shareholders,

  2) acts not in *good faith* involving intentional misconduct,

  3) improper distributions, or

  4) transactions from which the director derived an improper personal benefit.

In general, the articles must contain (but not as a permanent part of the articles) the corporate office's postal address, the names, residence and postal addresses of the directors and president, treasurer, and clerk, the fiscal year, and the name and business address of the resident agent.

Corporations: Exceptions to Liability Protections

Exceptions to the rule of limited liability

A creditor may enforce corporate liability against a shareholder in two situations.

Defective incorporation

If the incorporators fail to comply with the incorporation statute's mandatory requirements, individual owners are liable for corporate debts.

The Secretary of State's approval of the incorporation is conclusive evidence of a corporation's lawful existence.

The incorporation statute provides that persons purporting to act as or on behalf of a corporation knowing that was no incorporation shall be jointly and severally liable for liabilities created while so doing.

Piercing the corporate veil

There are circumstances when actions of a legally created corporation or its shareholders become the basis for permitting a creditor of the corporation to hold the shareholders or corporations created by those shareholders liable for the debts of the corporation.

Factors relevant to holding shareholders of a corporation liable for corporate debts are:

1) intermingling corporate and personal assets,

2) failing to keep corporate records, and

3) inadequately capitalizing the corporation.

Common ownership of several brother-sister corporations is not alone enough ground for piercing the corporate veil.

If brother-sister corporations intermingle corporate accounts, fail to keep adequate records of each corporation's distinct existence, have shared employees, are inadequately capitalized, or do not hold out each corporation to the public as separate enterprises, the court may find joint liability among a group of corporations.

Notes for active learning

Corporations: Control and Management in the Corporation

Exercise of corporate purposes and powers

The incorporation statute provides a corporation with an extensive group of express and implied powers, including the power to guarantee a parent, subsidiary, or affiliated corporation's debt.

These powers shall be possessed by any corporation incorporated unless the articles of incorporation expressly disavow those powers.

The articles of incorporation do not require an enumeration of corporate powers.

Ultra vires

Because corporations have broad powers, an act of the corporation is rarely in excess of those powers and not *ultra vires* (i.e., acting beyond legal authority).

The *ultra vires* nature of a corporate act can only be challenged in a proceeding by a shareholder against the corporation to enjoin such act, a proceeding by the corporation against a present, former director or officer alleging they acted beyond the powers of the corporation or in a proceeding brought by the attorney general.

Allocation of power between shareholders and directors

The articles of incorporation (articles of organization for an LLC) are the ultimate internal governing document, limited only by the State's corporation statute.

By-laws are the third source of authority and are operative if not in conflict with the statute or articles of incorporation.

The incorporation statute ordinarily provides the power to manage a corporation is vested in the board of directors even though the shareholders as a group own the corporation.

Individual directors and the board of directors, as a body, are independent of the shareholders.

The directors owe a separate fiduciary duty to the corporate entity.

Corporate officers are ordinarily elected by the board of directors, and the chief executive officer reports to the board of directors.

The incorporation statute provides an alternative for the management of nonpublic corporations.

By unanimous agreement of shareholders, incorporated into the articles of incorporation or by-laws of a corporation, a corporation can:

1) eliminate the board of directors or restrict its powers;

2) modify the requirement that distributions be proportionate to share ownership;

3) modify the rules for creating the directors and officers of the corporation;

4) alter the voting power by or between the shareholders and directors;

5) transfer to one or more shareholders or another person part of the authority to exercise corporate powers or manage the business;

6) require the dissolution of the corporation at the request of one or more shareholders upon the occurrence of a specified event or contingency.

The existence of such an agreement must be noted conspicuously on the front or back of shares of the corporation.

Absent an agreement, the shareholders' fundamental power base is their ability to elect and remove directors (under some circumstances).

Fundamental corporate changes such as mergers, acquisitions, and amendments to the articles of incorporation must be approved by the shareholders, usually by a majority vote.

Shareholders have the power to make, amend, and repeal the by-laws unless this power to amend the by-laws is vested in the board of directors by the articles or by-laws.

The shareholders could amend the articles to vest power to amend the by-laws in the shareholders and then amend them.

Corporations: Requirements of Directors

Directors of the corporation

Except as provided in the incorporation statute, a corporation must have as many directors as shareholders but only needs a minimum of three directors if there are more than three shareholders.

Directors need not be stockholders.

Incorporators appoint the initial directors.

After the incorporators appoint the initial directors, they are elected at the annual meeting of stockholders, usually for one year or until their successors are elected and qualified.

Directors may be elected for staggered terms up to three years, but at least one staggered term must end each year.

The incorporation statute provides that the shareholders or the remaining directors may fill the vacancy under the articles or the by-laws.

Election of directors

Unless another method is set forth in the articles of incorporation or bylaws, directors are elected by a plurality of the votes cast by the shares entitled to vote in the election at a shareholders' meeting at which a quorum is present.

This shareholder voting method permits the holders of a majority of voting stock to elect the directors.

This procedure permits each class to secure representation on the board of directors.

The articles of incorporation may permit voting by the class of stock.

Amendments to the articles of incorporation relating to classification can be made only with the approval of a majority of the shares in the affected class.

Removal of directors

A director, including a director appointed by the other directors, may be removed without cause by a vote of the majority of the shares entitled to vote for directors.

A director elected by a class may only be removed by a vote of the majority of the shares in the class, which elected them.

If cumulative voting is authorized, a director may not be removed by the shareholders if the number of votes sufficient to elect with cumulative voting vote against their removal.

A director may be removed for cause by other directors after reasonable notice and an opportunity to be heard.

Operation of the board of directors

Regular meetings of the board of directors may be held without notice if the time and place are fixed by the by-laws or by a director resolution.

Notice is required for a special meeting of the board of directors.

However, directors can waive notice.

An objection based on lack of notice of the meeting is waived if a director attends the meeting and does not object to the lack of notice.

Directors' meetings of the corporation can be held outside of the resident state.

Unless the by-laws prescribe a different percentage, a majority of the directors then in office constitute a quorum.

A majority of those present at a validly called meeting is an act of the board of directors if a quorum is present.

Directors can bind the corporation to contractual obligations beyond the directors' terms.

Each director must vote on matters based on independent judgment at the time of the meeting.

Before a meeting, a director may not enter into a binding agreement to vote a specific way on an issue.

A director must vote in person, although they can attend a meeting through telephone or other electronic means.

Proxy voting by directors is not permitted.

Directors may act without a meeting if all directors consent in writing with a document filed with the clerk of the corporation.

Directors serve without compensation unless there is an agreement by the directors that they shall be compensated.

Delegation of directors' powers

Even though the board has the statutory power to manage the corporation, it usually delegates the authority to run day-to-day operations to the officers whom it elects.

The board can delegate some authority to committees of directors constituted by the board.

However, the board must make major decisions of the corporation (e.g., corporate distributions, propose to issue stock or pay dividends, remove directors, amend by-laws, or buy back stock).

The fact that directors delegated an issue to a committee does not relieve the directors of their fiduciary duty of care.

General standards for directors and officers

A director and officer shall discharge their duties as a director, member of a committee, or as an officer:

1) in good faith;

2) with the care that a person in a like position would reasonably believe appropriate under similar circumstances; and

3) in a manner which the director or officer reasonably believes to be in the corporation's best interests.

A director may consider the interests of the corporation's suppliers, creditors, customers, economy of the state, region, country, and long- and short-term interests of the corporation and its shareholders in determining the best interest of the corporation.

In discharging their duties, directors may rely on information, opinions, reports, or statements of employees, legal counsel, public accountants, and committees of the board of directors if they do not have knowledge that makes such reliance unwarranted.

A director is not liable for action (or failure to act) if they performed their duties following these standards.

Director's conflict of interest

A conflict-of-interest transaction is where a director of the corporation has a material direct or indirect interest.

An indirect conflict occurs if the director has a material financial interest in the other party to the transaction.

A transaction is not voidable solely due to the director's interest if any of the following is true.

1) The material facts of the transaction and the director's interest were known to the board or a committee, and the board/committee approves/ratifies the transaction.

   Approval or ratification occurs if the transaction receives the affirmative vote of a majority of the disinterested directors' votes.

   Disinterested directors on the board/committee have no direct or indirect interest in the transaction, but the transaction may not be authorized/ratified by a single director.

2) The material facts of the transaction and the director's interest were disclosed or known to the shareholders, and the shareholders approved the transaction.

   Approval or ratification occurs if it receives the affirmative vote of a majority of shares entitled to vote who have no direct or indirect material interest in the transaction.

3) The transaction was fair to the corporation.

Loans to directors

A corporation may not loan to or guarantee a loan of a director of the corporation unless:

1) the loan or guarantee is approved by a majority of votes of the outstanding shares of all classes except for the shares owned by the benefited director, or

2) the board of directors determines that the loan or guarantee benefits the corporation and either approves the specific loan or a general plan of loans or guarantees.

Specific liabilities of corporate directors

Unless they have a good faith defense, directors and officers are jointly and severally liable by statute if they cause or authorize the corporation to engage in any of the following acts:

1) improperly issue stock;

2) make a dividend distribution prohibited by statute;

3) wrongfully deny shareholders information.

If a director pays more than their pro-rata share of a judgment, the director is entitled to contribution from the other negligent directors.

Officers of the corporation

The officers of a corporation required by statute are the president, clerk, and treasurer.

The clerk must reside in the state of formation unless a resident registered agent to receive service of process is appointed.

These officers and other offices described in the by-laws are appointed by the board or by such persons as the board delegates its appointing authority.

Authority of officers

An officer is an agent of the corporation.

Each officer has the authority and shall perform the duties set forth in the by-laws or to the extent consistent with the by-laws, the duties prescribed by the board of directors, or the direction of an officer authorized by the board of directors to prescribe the duties of other officers.

An officer can possess implied authority to act because of the general custom or practice of the company or because it is reasonably necessary to accomplish matters specifically delegated.

The president of a corporation or its general manager has implied authority to accomplish any act on behalf of the corporation in the usual and ordinary course of its business.

The treasurer has the authority to receive funds, make approved disbursements, and execute notes.

The clerk or secretary is authorized to keep the corporate books, records, and seal, certify resolutions and keep minutes of corporate meetings.

The president and treasurer acting together have the authority to execute a deed conveying real estate owned by the corporation without a specific corporate vote authorizing the conveyance.

The board of directors can ratify unauthorized acts of an officer.

The agency rules concerning apparent authority apply to corporate officers.

Vacancies and removal of board members

The board of directors may remove an officer at any time with or without cause.

Notes for active learning

Corporations: Fiduciary Duties of Officers and Directors

Corporate opportunity

A director or officer breaches their fiduciary duty of loyalty to the corporation if they purchase a corporate opportunity for personal use without first offering it to the corporation if reasonably foresee that the corporation would be interested in acquiring that opportunity.

To qualify as a business opportunity, the prospective business must be related to the corporation's existing business or a field that the corporation expressed interest in entering.

The prospective business would be a business opportunity if the board of directors expressed an interest in acquiring a business like the prospective business or had acquired such businesses in the past.

An important determinant of whether a particular transaction constitutes a business opportunity is whether the prospective seller approached the officer or director because of their status as an officer or director or whether the offer was made to the officer or director for reasons unrelated to their corporate position.

If a prospective acquisition is a business opportunity, the officer or director may not acquire it for their account until they offer it to the corporation and a disinterested majority of directors.

If there is no disinterested majority and a disinterested majority of shareholders, waive their rights to acquire the business.

If a corporation successfully shows an acquisition by an officer or director was a breach of the fiduciary duty of loyalty, the most common remedy is to hold that the officer and director hold the business in a constructive trust for the corporation's benefit.

Competing with the corporation

Unless a director or officer has entered a contract with the corporation that prohibits it, they may engage in a business in competition with the corporation provided the conduct competes with the business in good faith.

The following activities would be a breach of the officer or director's fiduciary duty to conduct the competing business in good faith:

    1) hiring employees of the corporation for the competing business;

    2) using corporate facilities to conduct the competing business;

    3) planning or conducting the competing business during periods when paid to work for the corporation;

    4) use of corporate assets; or

5) use of customer lists of the corporation or confidential information obtained while working for the corporation.

The remedies available to the corporation for breaches of fiduciary duty are damages or a constructive trust.

Unless a corporate officer has signed a non-competition agreement and they did not use corporate assets while working for the corporation to help launch their new business, they are not precluded, upon the termination of their employment, from:

1) competing with their former employer, or

2) from using the intangible knowledge and skill acquired while employed.

Shareholders

Concerning the management of the corporation, shareholders have the right to elect directors, amend the by-laws, and approve fundamental corporate changes; and ratify the director's actions when there is a conflict of interest.

Shareholders' meeting

A shareholders' meeting of a corporation shall be held annually inside or outside of the resident state per the by-laws to elect directors and conduct business specified in the notice of the meeting.

Special meetings of shareholders can be called by the board of directors, the president, or by holders of 10% of the corporation's stock and 40% of a public corporation.

Shareholders of record must be given at least seven days' written notice of the time, place, and purposes of the meeting, but notice may be waived in writing before or after the meeting.

Unless the articles of incorporation or by-laws provide, the quorum requirement for a shareholders' meeting is satisfied if there are a majority of shareholders present in person or by proxy entitled to vote on the matter.

If a class vote is required, the majority quorum required applies to shares in the affected class.

Shareholders may take corporate action without a meeting either by a unanimous vote of shareholders or if permitted by the articles of incorporation by shareholders having not less than the minimum number of votes necessary to act at a meeting at which all shareholders entitled to vote on the action are present and voting.

Shareholder voting

At a shareholder meeting, shareholders of record on the corporate books on the specified record date are the only shareholders entitled to vote.

The board of directors may fix a record date not more than 70 days before a meeting.

If no record date is set, the record date is the close of business on the day before the notice of the meeting is given, or if no notice is given, then the day before the meeting.

Unless the articles of incorporation provide that specific classes of shares hold disproportionate voting power, each share is entitled to one vote.

The articles of incorporation may deny voting rights to a particular class of stock or limit the matters on which the class is entitled to vote.

Holders of non-voting stock have the right to vote on amendments to the articles of incorporation that would adversely affect the rights of non-voting stock.

Stock on which there are unpaid overdue subscriptions may not vote.

Proxy voting

Shareholders may vote by written proxy, which designates an agent to vote their share per their instructions.

A proxy is an agency agreement.

Therefore, it is freely revocable unless coupled with an interest.

One joint owner may execute a proxy on behalf of all joint owners unless the co-owner affirmatively objects.

A proxy is not valid for more than six months and terminates at the end of the meeting for which it is given.

Shareholder voting trusts

Shareholders may arrange to vote their stock collectively by using shareholder voting trusts.

A voting trust is an arrangement by which shareholders transfer legal title to their shares to a trust known as a voting trust.

The trustee of that trust has the power to vote the stock following the voting trust agreement.

The trustee issues voting trust certificates to the shareholders as evidence of their equitable ownership of the share transferred and deposits them with the corporation.

The voting trust certificate holders are entitled to dividends and all other rights, except voting.

A voting trust agreement is valid for the period set by the voting trust agreement and may be extended by shareholders.

Voting trust certificates are freely transferable.

Shareholder voting agreements

A contract among shareholders by which each agrees to vote their shares in a designated fashion is valid and specifically enforceable if it is in writing and signed by the participating shareholders.

A voting agreement is valid for such a period as is specified in the agreement.

Shareholder's right to information

A shareholder has the statutory right to inspect minutes of shareholders' and directors' meetings, the articles of incorporation, the by-laws, and the stock and transfer records, including the names, addresses, and holdings of shareholders.

The corporation may defend against a shareholder's request for information by arguing that the shareholder's purpose is to sell the information or use it for a purpose not in their interest as a shareholder, such as acquiring more stock in the company.

A shareholder has additional rights based upon common law to inspect account books and other corporate records.

To exercise their common law right, the shareholder has the burden of proving the proper purpose and good faith.

Under the incorporation statute, a corporation shall furnish to its shareholders upon request annual financial statements that include a balance sheet and income statement.

Corporations: Special Problems of Close Corporations

Close corporations

Bar exam questions frequently test the specific rules applicable to close corporations.

The following characteristics define a close corporation:

> 1) a small number of stockholders;
>
> 2) lack of a ready market for the corporate stock; and
>
> 3) a substantial majority of stockholder's participation in the corporation's management, direction, and operations.

The articles of incorporation of a close corporation frequently contain provisions designed to protect the rights of minority shareholders.

A high quorum requirement for a director's meeting or a shareholder's meeting permits a minority shareholder/director to block action by refusing to attend meetings.

Provisions requiring supermajorities to pass specific resolutions permit a minority director to block action.

Classification of stock permits a class holder to preserve representation on the board of directors.

A provision giving stockholders pre-emptive rights to purchase their pro-rata share of new stock issues protects the minority shareholder from dilution.

Stock transfer restrictions for close corporations

Unless there is a provision in the articles of incorporation or by-laws or an agreement among shareholders restricting the transfer of shares, the shares are freely transferable.

The transfer of shares of a close corporation may be restricted by the articles of incorporation, bylaws, or an agreement among shareholders.

A stock transfer restriction must be noted on the certificate or sent to a shareholder holding stock without a certificate.

Unless noted, a transfer restriction is not enforceable against a person without knowledge of the restriction.

Restrictions on the transfer of shares are authorized to maintain the corporation's status under tax laws such as subchapter S, preserve exemptions under federal or state securities law, or other reasonable purpose.

A valid stock transfer restriction can

1) obligate the stockholder to first offer the restricted shares to the corporation or another person before selling them;

2) require the corporation or another person to acquire the restricted shares;

3) require the approval of the corporation or another person before the shares are transferred if that approval is not manifestly unreasonable; or

4) prohibit the transfer of restricted shares to designated persons or classes of persons if that prohibition is not manifestly unreasonable.

Fiduciary duty of close corporation shareholders

Shareholders in a close corporation owe a duty of the utmost good faith and loyalty.

Majority stockholders must demonstrate a legitimate business purpose for any action harming the minority shareholders.

Even if there is a business purpose, the minority shareholders are entitled to show that the corporations' objective could have been achieved through a less harmful alternative.

The fiduciary duty of shareholders in close corporations extends to minority shareholders and prohibits them from harming the corporation by vetoing necessary actions.

For example, a minority shareholder used the veto power over corporate action given in the articles of incorporation to prevent the declaration of dividends (e.g., this refusal led to substantial tax penalties for which the minority shareholder was held liable).

The majority shareholder's fiduciary duty to the minority shareholders has been applied to require the corporation to extend the same stock repurchase option to minority shares as was given to the majority shareholder.

The fiduciary duty of the majority shareholder to the minority shareholders has been used to prevent an unfair advantage from being given to the majority shareholders in the sale of assets or a merger (e.g., prevented the termination of a minority shareholder's employment with the corporation).

Ordinarily, a breach of fiduciary duty to the corporation in a close corporation must be brought by a shareholders' derivative action.

Where a derivative suit is inadequate, a direct suit by a shareholder who has been harmed by a breach of fiduciary duty by another shareholder has been permitted.

Duties of the controlling shareholders

Controlling shareholders in corporations owe a fiduciary duty to minority shareholders and cannot use their control to exploit the corporation or minority unfairly.

This duty is most apparent when the controlling shareholder sells its shares, which carries the right to manage the corporation.

If the controlling shareholder fails to exercise due care in picking a buyer and sells control to a party who uses control of the corporation to steal from it or another improper purpose, the selling controlling shareholder will be liable in a direct suit by harmed minority shareholders.

If the controlling shareholder merges the corporation with another corporation, the terms of the merger and related agreements that benefit the controlling shareholder (e.g., employment, consulting agreements) will be scrutinized to determine if the controlling shareholder received consideration from these collateral agreements.

Notes for active learning

Corporations: Securities Regulations

Improper trading in securities – state law

When a person with information derived from private, non-public sources within the corporation uses that information to profit on the corporation's stock, that activity may constitute a breach of fiduciary duty.

The corporation could sue to impose a constructive trust on profits derived from trades based upon such information.

This cause of action belongs to the corporation and requires no suit by the buyer or seller.

Federal law: Sections 10(b) and 16 and Rule 10b-5

There are extensive federal laws, notably Sections 10(b) and 16 of the Federal Securities Act of 1934 and Rule 10b-5, which implements Section 10(b), that regulate the use of inside information in the purchase and sale of securities.

Uniform Securities Act

The Uniform Securities Act prohibits fraud in the purchase or sale of securities or related advisory activities.

Broker-dealers and their agents must register with the Secretary of State.

Non-exempt securities must be registered with the Secretary of State before being sold or offered for sale.

Notes for active learning

Corporations: Shareholders and Member Litigation

Direct suits

If a shareholder is harmed in their capacity as a shareholder, they can bring a suit directly against the corporation.

For example, a holder of preferred stock could bring a suit to compel a dividend if the corporation failed to make payment when the terms of the preferred stock made such a payment mandatory.

If the remedy sought is for the corporation's benefit rather than the shareholder in their individual capacity, a direct suit is not permitted.

Derivative suits

A shareholder's capacity to bring derivative suits is heavily tested.

A shareholder files a derivative suit on behalf of the corporation to pursue a legal remedy that the corporation itself has failed to pursue.

A derivative suit is usually brought in the form of a class action on behalf of the plaintiff and other shareholders similarly situated.

Conditions precedent to commencing suit

A shareholder may not bring a derivative suit unless satisfying the following conditions.

1) The plaintiff must have been a shareholder at the time of the transaction, which is the subject matter of the suit, or own shares as the result of the operation of law (e.g., inheritance from a contemporaneous shareholder) and must fairly and adequately represent the interests of the corporation in enforcing their rights.

2) The plaintiff shareholder must make a written demand upon the corporation and wait 90 days to take suitable action.

If the directors refer the demand to the shareholders, the plaintiffs must wait 90 days after the shareholder demand is made.

Stay of the proceedings

If the corporation commences an inquiry into the allegations made in the demand or the complaint, the court can stay the proceedings for such time as it considers appropriate.

Dismissal

A shareholder derivative suit shall be dismissed if the demand required of directors or shareholders has been rejected and the vote to reject the demand was:

1) by a majority vote of the independent directors which constituted a quorum; or

2) a majority vote of a committee consisting of 2 or more independent directors, whether they constituted a quorum; or

3) the vote of the holders of a majority of the shares entitled to vote, not including shares of the shareholder whose wrongdoing is alleged.

A director is not disqualified as an independent director solely because they were nominated or elected by a person who is a defendant in the derivative proceeding or because they have been named a defendant in the derivative proceeding.

As part of a motion to dismiss, the corporation must file with the court a document showing the requisite votes and independence of the directors or shareholders casting them.

The plaintiff can challenge the document.

Discontinuance or settlement of a derivative suit

Court approval is required to discontinue or settle a derivative suit.

If the settlement substantially affects shareholders, the court can direct notice be sent to shareholders affected.

Upon termination of the suit, the court can order the corporation to pay counsel fees for the plaintiff and the defendant.

Other shareholders may move to intervene on the ground that they have an interest relating to the property or transaction; the outcome might impair their ability to protect that interest.

The request for intervention will be denied if the interest of the other shareholder is already adequately represented.

Indemnification of officers and directors

If the articles of incorporation or the By-laws adopted by the shareholders' permit, the corporation may indemnify present or former directors, officers, employees, or agents for the expenses related to defending themselves against shareholder suits for damages awarded against them or paid as a result of a settlement.

The corporation cannot indemnify such a defendant adjudicated not to have acted in good faith in the reasonable belief that their action was in the corporation's best interests.

Indemnification for the expenses of the lawsuit may be provided before the suit is finally adjudicated if the defendant undertakes to repay the advance if not entitled to it.

Corporations may take out an insurance policy to protect officers and directors from such lawsuits regardless of their power to indemnify them.

Notes for active learning

Corporations: Corporate Financial Structure

Debt securities

A debt security is a corporation's contractual obligation to repay borrowed money.

If designated a debenture, the obligation is unsecured.

A debt designated as a bond is usually an obligation secured by a security interest in specific corporate assets.

The debt instrument defines the holder's rights to interest repayment security and, in some cases, the right to convert the debt into specified equity securities.

Equity securities

Equity securities represent the ownership interest in the corporation.

The holders are entitled to profits and bear the economic burden of losses.

Each class of equity securities carries such voting rights, dividend rights, and liquidation rights as are delineated by the articles of incorporation.

Common stock

Its common stock represents the residual ownership interest of the corporation.

Its rights on liquidation are in the corporation's assets after debts have been paid, and the holders of all classes of stock having a liquidation preference have been satisfied.

Voting rights are usually vested in the holders of the common stock.

Common stock may be classified so that the voting rights of classes are differentiated.

Common stockholders have no right to dividends.

If there are classes of preferred stock, common stock dividends ordinarily cannot be paid until the dividend obligations to the preferred stock are satisfied.

Common stockholders are not entitled to a dividend unless declared by the directors after paying preferred stock dividends.

Preferred stock

Holders of preferred stock are entitled to receive a fixed dividend before common stockholders are paid.

Some preferred shares carry additional dividend rights, which permit those shares to participate in further dividend distributions.

Preferred stock may carry the right to a mandatory dividend if there are sufficient earnings.

Preferred dividends are usually cumulative so that back preferred dividends must be paid before holders of common stock are entitled to a dividend.

Ordinarily, preferred stock does not carry voting rights. The liquidation rights of preferred stock are ordinarily a fixed sum, representing par value.

Issuance of shares

Shares cannot be legally issued unless the articles of incorporation authorize them.

Once authorized, the stock may be issued by a vote of the shareholders or the board of directors if the board is authorized to issue stock by the by-laws or shareholders.

Stock subscriptions

A stock subscription is an offer by a prospective shareholder to purchase stock.

A stock subscription offer is irrevocable for six months unless the subscription agreement prescribes a different period.

The agreement is not binding on the corporation until accepted by the directors after the corporation is formed.

In accepting a stock subscription offer, directors can establish the payment terms.

If a subscriber fails to pay the demanded amount within 30 days after the due date, the corporation may auction their subscription rights and hold them liable for the difference.

In the alternative, the directors can specifically enforce the subscription contract by tendering the stock and suing for the amount due.

The corporation can accept payment for shares in cash, by a promissory note, by property transferred to the corporation, as services to the corporation which have already been performed, and contracts for services to be performed.

Before they issue shares, the directors must determine that the consideration to be paid for the shares is adequate. That determination, once made, is conclusive.

The concept of par value as the minimum amount which may be received for shares has been abolished even if shares state a par value.

Pre-emptive rights

Shareholders do not have pre-emptive rights, which entitle them to maintain their proportionate share of a corporation's stock in the event more stock is issued, unless pre-emptive rights are authorized by the articles or in a by-law adopted by and subject to amendment only by the shareholders.

Even if pre-emptive rights do not exist, if the directors vote to issue stock to deprive an existing shareholder of substantial rights, it is possible to enjoin that issuance because the directors are breaching a fiduciary duty to the plaintiff shareholder.

This is a likely result in a close corporation.

Share certificates

The shares of a corporation may be represented by certificates or held in electronic form.

The record of stock ownership is kept with the books of the corporation.

Unless the corporate by-laws specifically provide that no transfer of stock is effective until:

1) that transfer is recorded on the records of the corporation, or

2) unless there is a provision in the articles of incorporation or by-laws, which requires corporate approval before a shareholder can transfer their stock.

A transfer of stock is effective when a stockholder delivers their stock to a transferee with an appropriate endorsement authorizing a transfer on the books of the corporation.

A certificate will state the number of shares and the class to which the shares belong.

If the corporation has more than one class, the characteristics of that class must be noted on the certificate or refer to a description of these rights in the articles of incorporation.

If there are restrictions on stock transferability, for that restriction to be effective, it must be conspicuously noted on the certificate, or the stockholder must have actual notice of the restriction at the time they acquired the stock.

Notes for active learning

Corporations: Corporate Distributions

Corporate dividends – mechanics of payment

A dividend is a transfer of cash, property, or the corporation's stock from the corporation to shareholders in proportion to their stock ownership.

The directors ordinarily have uncontrolled discretion regarding the time and amount of a dividend payment.

Directors may be compelled to pay dividends by a direct suit by a shareholder against the corporation if the governing corporate documents or contractual obligations make the payment mandatory or if the directors have acted in bad faith.

Once the directors vote to pay a dividend, and that declaration is announced to the shareholders, the corporation is contractually obligated to pay the dividend.

When the directors declare a dividend, it is payable to shareholders who own the stock on a particular date, known as the record date, which may be fixed by the articles, by-laws, or resolution on a date no more than 60 days before payment.

Limitations on the payment of dividends

If a corporation would not be able to pay its existing and reasonably foreseeable debts when they become due, or the corporation is insolvent in that its total assets would be less than the sum of its total liabilities, it may not pay a dividend

A corporation cannot pay a dividend if the articles of incorporation forbid the payment.

Liability of directors for improper payments of dividends

Directors are jointly and severally liable for an illegal dividend paid unless they relied in good faith upon corporate financial records.

A director liable for an illegal dividend is entitled to contribution from other negligent directors.

A shareholder must repay an illegal dividend to the corporation.

Redemption of shares

Holders of some classes of stock, usually preferred stock, can be compelled to sell their shares to the corporation for a specific price at the option of the corporation.

This forced sale is a *right of redemption* and must be stated when the stock class is described in the articles of incorporation.

If the corporation decides to redeem only a portion of the stock eligible for redemption, it must redeem pro-rata.

Once a corporation votes to redeem stock and notifies the shareholder, a contract to purchase has been formed, and the shareholder can sue for the redemption price.

Repurchase of corporate shares

If the corporation is solvent, and the repurchase will not render it insolvent, and it is not contractually prohibited for doing so, a corporation can contract with its shareholders to repurchase its shares at a mutually agreeable price.

In a close corporation, the controlling shareholders have a fiduciary duty to repurchase shares from minority shareholders to the same extent and at the same price at which they are repurchasing shares from the majority shareholders.

Reacquired shares are treated as authorized but unissued shares and can be reissued in the manner that unissued stock can be issued.

The concept of treasury stock has been abolished.

Corporations: Fundamental Corporate Changes

Amendment of the articles of incorporation

Articles of amendment must be submitted to the board of directors and approved by them.

The articles of incorporation can be amended by the addition or deletion of provisions. The articles as reconstituted are still valid by a two-thirds vote of the shareholders and a separate two-thirds vote of a specific class of stock if that class of stock is adversely affected.

The articles of amendment must be filed with the Secretary of State within 60 days of the shareholders' vote.

The amendment takes effect on filing unless a later date within 30 days of the filing is specified.

The following amendments only require a majority vote:

> an increase or reduction of an authorized class,
>
> changes in par value, or
>
> a change of corporate name.

If an amendment is adopted, which adversely affects a stockholder's rights, they are entitled to be paid for the appraised value of their stock before the amendment.

Appraisal and redemption rights are triggered by:

1) the alteration or termination of a preferential or pre-emptive right; or

2) creation, alteration, or termination of redemption rights or transfer restriction; or

3) the termination of any voting right.

Mergers and consolidations

A merger occurs when one of two existing corporations is absorbed by another.

If two corporations combine into one new corporation, the result is a consolidation.

A merger (or consolidation) requires each corporation's agreement to adopt a merger plan (or consolidation).

Unless the surviving corporation owns 90% of the stock of the acquired corporation, or unless the surviving corporation is issuing less than 15% of its outstanding shares in the merger, written notice must be given to shareholders of both corporations, whether or not entitled to vote, at least 20 days before the shareholder's meeting. Two-thirds of each class entitled to vote must approve the plan.

A class adversely affected is entitled to vote and must be approved by a two-thirds vote.

If the articles of incorporation permit it, a vote of fewer than two-thirds of the shareholders is enough to approve a merger as long as a majority of shareholders approve.

Once the articles of the merger are approved, they must be filed in the Secretary of State's office and in the registry of deeds in each district in which real property is located.

Dissenting shareholders are entitled to appraisal rights (below).

Sale of all corporate assets

Shareholder approval by a two-thirds vote is required for a corporation to sell or lease, but not to mortgage or pledge, substantially all its assets.

A dissenting shareholder is entitled to appraisal rights.

Appraisal rights

A shareholder of a corporation merging or selling its assets is entitled to appraisal rights.

To qualify for the rights, an eligible shareholder must file a written objection to the merger or sale with the corporation before the shareholders' meeting is called to approve the transaction.

This shareholder cannot vote in favor of the plan.

If a shareholder has complied with these conditions, they must make a written demand on the corporation to purchase their shares at fair value within 20 days after notice of shareholder approval of the plan.

Within 50 days from the meeting date, the corporation must pay a fair value of their stock.

If the corporation and dissenter disagree on the stock value, either may file for a judicial determination of value within four months after the expiration date required for payment.

Dissenting shareholders are made parties to that litigation.

The court determines the shares' value on the day preceding the vote approving the action and adds interest to the award.

Dissolution of the corporation

Dissolution terminates the existence of a corporation. Corporate existence continues for three years after the dissolution to settle matters concerning the corporation.

Judicial dissolution is granted in response to a petition by a majority of stockholders or 40% of the stockholders if:

1) the directors are deadlocked, and the shareholders cannot break the deadlock, or

2) the shareholders are deadlocked and have not elected successors for directors whose terms have expired, and dissolution is in the shareholders' best interests.

A corporation can voluntarily dissolve by filing with the Secretary of State articles of dissolution approved by a two-thirds vote of each class outstanding and entitled to vote thereon.

The Secretary of State will involuntarily dissolve a corporation:

which has not filed required reports or taxes for two years, or

if the State Secretary is satisfied that it is inactive, or

if its dissolution would be in the public interest.

The Secretary of State may revive a dissolved corporation irrespective of the time elapsed or dissolution method.

Takeover bids

The incorporation statute limits a person's right to carry out a hostile takeover of a corporation by acquiring stock in that corporation without the approval of management.

A person attempting a takeover must file information with the company and the Secretary of State and provide public notice before attempting to gain control of more than ten percent of any class of securities of a target company.

The offer must be on the same terms and conditions to all shareholders.

Any shareholder holding at least five percent of a corporation's voting stock is prohibited from carrying out a merger, consolidation, sale of at least ten percent of corporate assets, recapitalization, or certain other business combinations with the corporation if the shareholder has been such an interested shareholder for less than three years unless the board approved the shareholder's acquisition of a five percent interest or such a business combination before the shareholder became interested.

Conflict of laws

Internal corporate affairs are governed by statute regardless of where a suit may arise.

Professional corporations

Persons incorporate to render professional services such as legal or medical services.

Only licensed professionals can hold stock in such a corporation.

Tax status of the corporation

The tax status of a corporation occurs if it has three of the following four characteristics:

1) continuity of life;

2) centralization of management;

3) liability for corporate debts limited to corporate property; and

4) free transferability of interest.

Limited Liability Company (LLC)

Limited Liability Companies

The Limited Liability Company Act authorizes the limited liability company (LLC).

The LLC is a combination of a corporation's characteristics and a limited partnership.

Like stockholders of a corporation, the LLC members enjoy limited liability.

The organization is taxed as a partnership rather than a corporation taxed under subchapter C of the Internal Revenue code.

Limited liability companies have been held to lack continuity of life and free transferability of interest and can be taxed as a partnership.

Limited Liability Company formation

An authorized person must execute the certificate of organization (i.e., articles of organization) and deliver it to the Secretary of State to form an LLC.

The articles of organization are for an LLC, like the articles of incorporation (i.e., corporate charter) are for a corporation.

The certificate of organization must contain the information required in the articles of a corporation (e.g., name, purpose, address, agent).

If there is a date when the company will be dissolved, it must be stated.

The articles of organization must state if the company is to be managed by managers and set forth their names and addresses.

If managed by members, their names and addresses must be listed.

The words limited liability company (or LLC) must be the last words of the name.

Powers of the Limited Liability Company

A limited liability company has the power to carry on any lawful business (same manner and same extent) as a business corporation.

Management of the Limited Liability Company

In the absence of an operating agreement, the management of a limited liability company shall be vested in its members.

An LLC is like a general partnership, except that if an operating agreement does not provide for members' voting rights, the decision of members of the limited liability company who own more than fifty percent of the unreturned contributions shall be controlling.

The statute defines unreturned contributions as the agreed value, as stated in the company's records of each member's contributions to the extent the company has received them.

An operating agreement governs the affairs of a limited liability company in most cases.

The operating agreement may designate the managers of a limited liability company and set out their powers, their terms of office, and how they are elected.

The operating agreement may prescribe the rights and obligations of classes of members and how they vote in the same manner as the articles of incorporation (corporate charter) address these issues for corporations.

Contributions of capital to the Limited Liability Company

The capital contributions to an LLC are like stock subscriptions in a corporation.

A member's contributions to the company's capital may consist of cash or other property, services rendered, or a promissory note or other obligation to contribute cash or property or perform services.

If the member fails to contribute the cash or property promised, the defaulting member can be required to pay cash in place of the property or services, is personally liable to creditors who rely on the promise to contribute capital and can be stripped of their interest in the LLC.

Limited Liability Company property

A limited liability company is an entity much like a corporation.

A limited liability company has the power to own, manage, and transfer property.

Instruments relating to the company's real property are binding upon the company if executed by a person identified in the articles of organization as a person authorized to execute such documents on behalf of the company.

Distribution of property

Like a corporation pays dividends, the limited liability company may, from time to time, distribute property to the members upon the basis stipulated in the operating agreement.

Nature and transferability of member's interest

Much like an interest in the stock of a corporation, a member's interest in a limited liability company is personal property.

The operating agreement can provide how the members transfer or assign interests.

A member's interest in a limited liability company can be transferred like transferring a partnership interest.

Unless members who are not disposing of their interest approve of the proposed transfer (or assignment) by unanimous written consent, or there is compliance with a procedure provided for in the written operating agreement, the transferee of a member's interest has no right to participate in the management or become a member in the company.

The transferee is entitled to receive only the share of profits or income compensation and the return of contributions to which that member otherwise would be entitled.

Liability of the LLC member to the company

A member is personally liable to a limited liability company for:

1) the difference between contributions to capital which have been made and the amount stated in the articles of organization as having been made; and

2) unpaid future contribution to capital, which they agreed in the articles to make with conditions stated in the articles.

A limited liability company can reduce or cancel a member who fails to contribute.

These liabilities may be waived or compromised only by the consent of all members.

However, even if the members execute a waiver, the right of a creditor of the limited liability company to enforce the liability is unaffected if the creditor extended credit or if their claim arose after the filing and before cancellation or amendment of the articles.

Liability for company's obligation

A limited liability company offers members similar limited liability protection as a corporation to the shareholders.

Parties to actions

Concerning litigation, a member of an LLC is similar as a shareholder of a corporation.

The LLC member is not a proper party in litigation for or against the company except when the object enforces a member's right against or liability to the company.

Process against the company may be served as if the company were a partnership or upon the registered agent at their business address.

Comparing an LLC with a subchapter S corporation

A limited liability company is like an S Corporation as closely held corporations can elect to avoid taxation as a corporation if they comply with limitations.

A limited liability company avoids these limitations.

In an S corporation, there can be no more than seventy-five shareholders; a limited liability company has no limitation on the number of members.

Only U.S. citizens or resident aliens can be shareholders in an S corporation.

Foreign nationals who are not resident aliens can be members of a limited liability company.

An S corporation shareholder may write off depreciation losses and other deductions only to the extent of their basis in the stock.

In a limited liability company, losses can be claimed more than the investment.

Dissolution of a Limited Liability Company

A limited liability company is dissolved in substantially the same manner as a corporation.

Comparison of LLC and Pass-Through Entities

	Limited Liability Company	Limited Partnership	S-Corporation
Limited liability	Members have protection from Limited Liability Company's debts.	Limited partners protected from partnership's debts. None for general partner.	Shareholders have protection from corporate debt.
Management participation	No restrictions	Participation only by general partner. Participating limited partners void limited liability.	No restrictions
Transferability of ownership	Restrictions imposed by statute to avoid corporate *"transferability of interest."*	Restrictions imposed by the *partnership agreement*.	Restrictions if destroys "S" election or other.
Continuity	Restrictions by statute to avoid corporate attribute of *"continuity of life."*	Restrictions imposed by the *partnership agreement*.	Continuity of life.
Tax status	Yes, federal *check box classification*. Yes, most states adopt check box system.	Yes, federal check box classification. Yes, most states adopt check box system.	Lost if transfer to investors making the corporation ineligible for "S" tax treatment.
Number of owners	At least 1 with a few states requiring 2 or more.	At least one general partner and one limited partner.	1 to 100 shareholders
Types of owners	Unrestricted	Unrestricted	U.S. residents and citizens, estates, and certain trusts.
Classes of ownership	Multiple stock classes	Multiple stock classes	One, with same or different voting.

Organizational costs	General fees and expenses for each pass-through entity	General fees and expenses for each pass-through entity	General fees and expenses for each pass-through entity
Income and loss	Allocation	Allocation	No allocation
Deductibility of losses	Members may deduct their allowable share only to the extent of tax basis in the LLC interest, includes allocable LLC debt.	Partners deduct partnership loss to basis in partnership, includes allowable partnership debt.	Shareholders may deduct share of loss to the extent of tax basis. Corp. debt not a factor.
Passive loss rules	Members who materially participate are not subject to passive loss rules. Others are subject to passive loss rules.	General partner materially participates is not subject to passive loss rules. Limited partners are subject to passive loss rules.	Shareholders who materially participate are not subject to passive loss rules. Others are subject to passive loss rules.
Self-employment tax	Members subject to self-employment tax.	General partners subject to self-employment. Limited partners are not.	Shareholders may be subject to self-employment tax.

Business Corporations

Corporations are the most dominant form of business organization in the United States, generating more than 85 percent of the country's gross business receipts. Corporations range in size from one owner to thousands of owners. Owners of corporations are shareholders. A corporation is a separate legal entity for most purposes. Corporations are treated, in effect, as artificial persons created by the state. They can sue or be sued in their names, enter into and enforce contracts, hold title to and transfer property, and be found civilly and criminally liable for law violations. Corporations cannot be imprisoned, so the usual criminal penalty assesses a fine, revokes licenses and other sanctions.

Corporations have the following unique characteristics:

Limited liability of shareholders: as separate legal entities, corporations are liable for their debts. The shareholders have liability that only extends to their investments.

Free transferability of shares. Corporate shares are freely transferable by the shareholder by sale, assignment, pledge, or gift unless issued according to certain exemptions from securities registration.

Perpetual existence. Corporations exist in perpetuity unless a specific duration is stated in the corporation's articles of incorporation. The shareholders can voluntarily terminate the existence of a corporation. Creditors may involuntarily terminate corporations if an involuntary bankruptcy petition is granted. The death, insanity, or bankruptcy of a shareholder, director, or officer does not affect its existence.

Centralized management: the board of directors (BOD) makes policy decisions concerning the corporation's operation. The shareholders elect members of the board of directors. The directors then appoint corporate officers to run the day-to-day operations. Together, the directors and officers form the corporate "management."

Notes for active learning

Relationship matrix

Notes for active learning

Review Questions

Multiple-choice questions

1. The most dominant form of business organization in the U.S. is the:

A. Partnership

B. Proprietorship

C. Limited Partnership

D. Corporation

2. The Securities and Exchange Commission (SEC) was created in:

A. 1889

B. 1934

C. 1948

D. 1992

3. Title VII prohibits employment discrimination in:

I. Decisions regarding promotion

II. Compensation

III. Merit-based advancements

A. I only

B. I and II only

C. II only

D. II and III only

4. The partners in a limited liability partnership are liable for the debts of the LLP:

A. Beyond their investment

B. Not beyond their investment

C. 150% of their investment

D. 50% of their investment

5. The following are exceptions to the rule that a principal is NOT liable for the independent contractor's torts EXCEPT:

A. Nondelegable duties

B. Unreasonably dangerous activities

C. Negligence *per se*

D. Negligence selection of an independent contractor

6. What type of corporation can avoid double taxation?

I. C corporation

II. LLC corporation

III. S-corporation

A. I and II only

B. II and III only

C. III only

D. I, II and III

7. The form of ADR that involves a neutral party helping resolve the dispute without making a substantive decision on the merits is:

A. Arbitration

C. Mediation

B. Conciliation

D. Minitrials

8. The "coming and going" rule says that principals are generally not liable for injuries caused by their agents and employees on their way to:

A. The bathroom

C. A business lunch

B. A business meeting

D. To work

9. Businesses organized in the U.S. are subject to:

    I. U.S. laws

    II. Ethical duties in the conduct of its affairs

    III. Laws of countries where they operate

A. I and II only

C. I and III only

B. II only

D. I, II and III

10. A limited liability company (LLC) is most like the following organizations:

A. A sole proprietorship

C. A limited liability partnership

B. A general partnership

D. A corporation

11. Which of the following is NOT a characteristic of a corporation?

A. Limited liability of shareholders

C. Pass-through taxation

B. Perpetual existence

D. Centralized management

12. The type of bankruptcy known as straight bankruptcy is:

A. Chapter 7

C. Chapter 11

B. Chapter 9

D. Chapter 13

13. The document governing the internal management of a corporation is the:

A. Articles of Incorporation

C. Meeting minutes

B. Executive agreement

D. Bylaws

14. A Securities and Exchange Commission (SEC) registration statement must contain:

    I. The securities offered for sale

    II. The registrant's business

    III. Pending litigation

A. I and II only   **C.** II and III only

B. II only   **D.** I, II and III

15. Business organizations include all but the following:

A. Limited liability corporation   **C.** S-corporation

B. Limited liability partnership   **D.** Sole proprietorship

16. A bait and switch is a method to deceive:

    I. lenders

    II. consumers

    III. suppliers

A. I only   **C.** II and III only

B. II only   **D.** I, II and III

17. The following jobs are likely performed by independent contractors EXCEPT:

A. A lawyer   **C.** An electrician

B. A district manager   **D.** None of the above

18. This is NOT an advantage of a sole proprietorship:

A. Forming the company is easy and low cost

B. The sole proprietor is not responsible for the company's debts

C. The sole proprietor makes the decisions

D. The sole proprietor receives the profits

19. To file a Chapter 13 bankruptcy petition, the debtor must:

A. Have regular income   **C.** Be prepared to pay their debts

B. Have no secured debt   **D.** Be prepared to lose their assets

20. *Caveat emptor* means:

A. Let the seller beware

B. Let the buyer beware

C. Limited liability

D. Imminent danger

21. A corporation incorporated in Delaware but doing business in Hawaii is a(n):

A. Foreign corporation

B. Alien corporation

C. Domestic corporation

D. Subrogated corporation

22. The following is exempt property of the bankruptcy estate:

A. College loans

B. A primary automobile

C. A 2.5-carat engagement ring

D. Alimony

23. An employee in a factory injured by their employer's negligence may sue:

A. The worker's compensation board

B. The employer

C. The factory's landlord

D. None of the above

24. A Chapter 11 bankruptcy petitions are filed mostly by:

A. Corporations

B. Partnerships

C. Individuals

D. Sole Proprietorships

25. The agreement to form a partnership may be:

    I. Oral

    II. Written

    III. Implied

A. I only

B. I and II only

C. II and III only

D. I, II and III

26. Insider trading can be committed by:

    I. The CEO of a publicly traded company

    II. The temporary employee of a publicly traded company

    III. An employee of a sole proprietorship

A. I only

B. I and II only

C. II and III only

D. I, II and III

27. A partnership may exist:

    I. For a fixed term

    II. For a set period

    III. Until some event occurs

A. I only   **C.** I and III only

B. I and II only   **D.** I, II and III

28. During which period of the registration an issuer may sell the offered securities?

A. The prefiling period   **C.** The post-effective period

B. The waiting period   **D.** The intermediary period

29. All of the following assets are securities EXCEPT:

A. Mineral rights   **C.** Houses

B. Debentures   **D.** Stocks

30. The owners of a corporation are the:

A. Board of directors   **C.** Shareholders

B. Officers   **D.** Members

31. In a Chapter 7 bankruptcy, the highest priority claim is:

A. Child support obligations   **C.** Federal taxes

B. Wages earned by employees   **D.** Secured creditors

32. The type of bankruptcy for business reorganization is Chapter:

A. 7   **C.** 11

B. 9   **D.** 13

33. The following may be general or limited partners:

    I. Natural persons

    II. Partnerships

    III. Corporations

A. I and II only   **C.** II and III only

B. II only   **D.** I, II and III

34. Which agency prosecutes those charged with violating the Securities Act?

A. The Securities and Exchange Commission

B. The Justice Department

C. The Federal Securities Enforcement Agency

D. The National Department of Securities

35. A prospectus is designed for:

A. Accountants

B. Investors

C. Attorneys

D. Judges

36. The common form of alternative dispute resolution in commercial disputes is:

A. Arbitration

B. Conciliation

C. Mediation

D. Private judging

37. General partners of a limited partnership have:

A. No liability

B. Limited liability

C. Unlimited liability

D. Defined liability

38. An agency may arise in the following way:

    I. Express agency

    II. Apparent agency

    III. Agency by ratification

A. I and II only

B. I and III only

C. III only

D. I, II and III

39. Agency relationships are formed by:

    I. Agents

    II. Principals

    III. Testators

A. I only

B. II only

C. I and II only

D. I, II and III

40. Which of the following events terminates an agency?

    I. Mutual agreement

    II. Lapse of time

    III. Purpose achieved

A. I only   **C.** III only

B. II only   **D.** I, II and III

41. Businesses consist of all but the following types of employment relationships?

A. Employer-employee   **C.** Master-servant

B. Principal-agent   **D.** None of the above

42. In an undisclosed agency, when the third party is not aware of the agency or the principal:

A. The principal is not liable for the contract with the third party

B. The agent is not liable for the contract with the third party

C. The principal and the agent are both liable for the contract with the third party

D. Any contract would be void, so there would be no liability as to it

43. Agency by ratification occurs when:

    I. A person misrepresents themselves as an agent but is not

    II. The purported principal ratifies the unauthorized act of the agent

    III. The agent and principal have a long-standing relationship

A. I only   **C.** II and III only

B. I and II only   **D.** I, II and III

44. Respondeat superior means:

A. Follow legal commands   **C.** Let the buyer beware

B. Let the master answer   **D.** Use caution while proceeding

True/false questions

45. A corporation is the simplest form of business organization.

      True   False

46. The certificate of limited partnership must be filed with the local government.

      True   False

47. General partners are personally liable for the debts of the partnership.

      True   False

48. The Securities Exchange Act regulates the conduct of brokerage companies but not publicly traded companies.

      True   False

49. The sole proprietor has limited liability for contracts of the company.

      True   False

50. Limited partners participate in the management but not the financing of the partnership.

      True   False

51. A manufacturing facility is an example of a stationary source of air pollution.

      True   False

52. A partnership agreement may NOT be created implicitly.

      True   False

53. The SEC has the power to prohibit the issuance of securities due to an insufficient registration statement.

      True   False

54. The issuer may be a new company offering securities to the public through an initial public offering (IPO).

      True   False

55. The Securities and Exchange Commission is a specific government regulation.

      True   False

56. The primary purpose of bankruptcy laws is to have debtors pay creditors.

    True   False

57. A sole proprietorship protects the owner from limited liability.

    True   False

58. General partners are personally liable for the debts of the partnership.

    True   False

59. Limited partners give up their right to profits in exchange for limited liability.

    True   False

60. General partnerships must have a written partnership agreement.

    True   False

61. The federal securities laws came about after the stock market crash.

    True   False

62. A partner cannot violate the terms of the partnership agreement and withdraw and dissolve the partnership at any time.

    True   False

63. A sole proprietorship is the simplest form of business organization.

    True   False

64. Common stock qualifies as a security under the SEC definition, but preferred stock does not.

    True   False

65. A limited liability partnership (LLP) can exist without a general partner.

    True   False

66. The Federal Trade Commission (FTC) regulates the labeling of consumer goods.

    True   False

67. If an investor owns shares in Apple, they do not register with the SEC before reselling those shares.

       True   False

68. The Food and Drug Administration has authority over cosmetic products.

       True   False

69. The Consumer Product Safety Commission is a private, nonprofit organization.

       True   False

70. To sustain a case of false and deceptive advertising, the FTC needs to prove that the ad in question deceived consumers.

       True   False

71. Assuming more than two partners, a person may be a general and a limited partner in the same limited partnership.

       True   False

72. The Superfund legislation provides that the owner of a property containing hazardous waste can be liable for clean-up costs, even if they were not at fault in disposing of the waste.

       True   False

73. Insider trading occurs when anyone buys or sells stock based on nonpublic information.

       True   False

74. Limited partners are liable for the debts of the partnership.

       True   False

75. States do not have securities laws.

       True   False

76. Someone who is an employee-at-will cannot sue for wrongful discharge.

       True   False

77. Federal environmental protection law prohibits businesses from polluting the air.

       True   False

78. An employee is typically an agent of the employer.

  True   False

79. A party who employs another to act on their behalf is known as an *agent*.

  True   False

80. In an undisclosed agency, the agent is not liable to the third-party with whom the agent has transacted business.

  True   False

81. The principal is not liable for injuries caused by their agents while they travel to and from work.

  True   False

82. There are no significant liability differences between a principal-agent and a principal-independent contractor relationship.

  True   False

83. Agency contracts created for illegal purposes are enforceable.

  True   False

84. A nonlawyer may not be appointed as an attorney-in-fact.

  True   False

85. Limited liability of agents for contracts involves disclosures made by the agent.

  True   False

86. In a partially disclosed agency, the agent is not liable to the party with whom the agent has transacted on behalf of the principal.

  True   False

87. When an agent terminates an agency, it is known as revocation of authority.

  True   False

88. The party that agrees to act on behalf of another is the principal.

  True   False

89. The principal-agent relationship is commonly referred to as an association.

      True   False

90. In an agency by ratification, the principal approves of the agent's unauthorized act.

      True   False

91. There is an implied-in-fact contract that can be an exception to employment-at-will.

      True   False

92. The principal's actions bind the principal in an apparent agency.

      True   False

Answer keys

1: D	11: C	21: A	31: D	41: C
2: B	12: A	22: D	32: C	42: C
3: B	13: D	23: D	33: D	43: D
4: B	14: D	24: A	34: B	44: B
5: C	15: A	25: D	35: B	
6: C	16: B	26: B	36: A	
7: C	17: B	27: D	37: C	
8: D	18: B	28: C	38: D	
9: D	19: A	29: C	39: C	
10: D	20: B	30: C	40: D	

45: False	61: True	77: False
46: False	62: False	78: False
47: True	63: True	79: False
48: False	64: False	80: False
49: False	65: True	81: True
50: False	66: True	82: False
51: True	67: True	83: False
52: False	68: True	84: False
53: True	69: False	85: True
54: True	70: False	86: False
55: False	71: True	87: False
56: False	72: True	88: False
57: False	73: False	89: False
58: True	74: False	90: True
59: False	75: False	91: True
60: False	76: False	92: True

Notes for active learning

Bar Exam Information, Preparation
and
Test-Taking Strategies

Introduction to the Uniform Bar Examination (UBE)

Structure of the UBE

The Uniform Bar Examination (UBE) includes 1) the Multistate Bar Examination (MBE), 2) Multistate Essay Examination (MEE), and 3) Multistate Performance Test (MPT).

The MBE has 200 multiple-choice questions accounting for 50% of the UBE.

The MEE has six essays worth 30% of the UBE score.

The MPT has two legal tasks (e.g., complaint, client letter) for 20% of the UBE score.

The Multistate Bar Examination (MBE)

The Multistate Bar Examination consists of 200 four-option multiple-choice questions prepared by the National Conference of Bar Examiners (NCBE).

Of these 200 questions, 175 are scored, and 25 are unscored pretest questions.

Candidates answer 100 questions in the three-hour morning session and the remaining 100 questions in the three-hour afternoon session.

The 175 scored questions are distributed with 25 questions on each of the seven subject areas: Federal Civil Procedure, Constitutional Law, Contracts, Criminal Law and Procedure, Evidence, Real Property, and Torts.

A specified percentage of questions in each subject tests topics in those subjects.

For example, approximately one-third of Evidence questions test hearsay and its exceptions, while approximately one-third of Torts questions test negligence.

Interpreting the UBE score report

Overall score. The National Conference of Bar Examiners (NCBE) states the Uniform Bar Exam (UBE) requires a passing scaled score between 260 to 280. Scores above 280 receive a passing score in every UBE state.

The "percentile" is the number of people that scored lower. If an examinee scored in the 47th percentile, they scored higher than 47% of the examinees (and lower than 53%).

The examinee is first given a "raw score,"; based on the number of correct answers.

The raw score is adjusted by adding points to achieve the "scaled score." The number of points added is determined by a formula that compares the difficulty of the current exam to prior benchmark exams.

The comparative performance of examinees on "control questions" (prior pretest questions) given on previous exams form the basis for determining each exam's difficulty.

MBE scaled score. Examinees receive a scaled score and not an MBE "raw" score (i.e., the number of correct answers). MBE scores are scaled scores calculated by the NCBE through a statistical process used for standardized tests.

According to the NCBE, this statistical process adjusts raw scores on the current exam to account for differences in difficulty compared to previously administered exams. The scaled score is calculated from the raw score, but the NCBE does not publish the conversion formula.

Since the MBE is a scaled score, equating makes it impossible to know precisely how many questions must be answered correctly to receive a particular score. Equating allows scores from different exams to be compared since a specific scaled score represents the same level of knowledge among exams.

The MBE is curved, so just because a score is "close" to passing does not mean you are close. For example, a 124 may be in the 31st percentile and a 136 in the 62nd percentile. A 12-point difference in scaled scores equates to a 31-point percentile difference. If you are in the 120s, much preparation is needed to increase your score.

For most states, aim for a scaled score of 135 to "pass" the MBE. If you are unsure what score you need, divide the passing score by two. For example, if a 270 is needed to pass the bar, divide 268 by two to yield 135 as a threshold score on the MBE.

The importance of the MBE score

A passing MBE score depends on the jurisdiction. In jurisdictions that score on a 200-point scale, the passing score is the overall score. Passing scores are often approximately 135.

For the July 2020 bar exam, the national average MBE score was 146.1, an increase of 5 points from the July 2019 national average of 141.1.

For comparison, on the July 2018 bar, the national average MBE score was 139.5, a decrease of about 2.2 points from the July 2017 national average of 141.7.

How much the MBE contributes depends on the jurisdiction. Each jurisdiction has its policy for the relative weight given to the MBE compared to other bar exam components.

For Uniform Bar Examination (UBE) jurisdictions, the MBE component is 50%.

Most jurisdictions combine the MBE score with the state essay exam score.

The overall state candidates' performance on the MBE controls the raw state essay's conversion to scaled scores. Achieve a scaled MBE score of at least 135 to pass the bar.

MEE and MPT scores

In a UBE score report, there are six scores for the Multistate Essay Exam (MEE) and two for the Multistate Performance Test (MPT). Most states release this information.

Most states grade on a 1–6 scale (some use another scale).

In states grading on a 1–6 scale, 4 is considered a passing score.

The MEE and MPT sections are not weighted equally.

The MEE essays are worth 60%, while the MPT is 40% of the written score.

Many examinees assume that they passed the MPT and MEE portions of the exam. Examine the score report to see how you performed on these portions.

The objective of the Multistate Bar Exam

Working knowledge of the MBE objectives, the skills it tests, how it is drafted, the relationship of the parts of an MBE question, and the testing limitations provide you a substantial advantage in choosing the correct answers to MBE questions and passing the bar.

Knowing which issues are tested and the form in which they are tested makes it more manageable to learn the large body of substantive law.

The MBE's fundamental objective is to measure fairly, and efficiently which law school graduates have the necessary academic qualifications to be admitted to the bar and exceed this threshold.

The multiple-choice exam used to accomplish this objective must be of a consistent level of difficulty.

The level at which the pass decision is made must be achievable by most candidates.

The MBE tests the following skills:

- reading carefully and critically
- identifying the legal issue in a set of facts
- knowing the law that governs the legal issues tested
- distinguish between frequently confused closely-related principles
- making reasonable judgments from ambiguous facts
- understanding how limiting words make plausible-sounding choices wrong
- choosing the correct answer by intelligently eliminating incorrect choices

Notes for active learning

Preparation Strategies for the Bar Exam

An effective bar exam study plan

There are a lot of great ideas about how to prepare. Follow through with these ideas and turn them into persistent action for successful preparation.

A detailed and well-planned study schedule has benefits, such as giving you a sense of control and building confidence and proficiency.

Pick a date about 12-14 weeks before the exam (November for the February exam and April for the July exam) and use it as the start of your active study period.

Start a month earlier than many others to have a month to review as final preparation at the end.

Students have found this effective. Use an elongated prep period as a study schedule.

Most examinees prefer at least two weeks before the exam to review the material.

By planning early, you will have more time. You may want three or four final weeks to review subjects, take timed exams, and ensure that you are prepared to take the exam.

A few notes on schedule management:

> Do not *start* memorizing during your initial review period. You should be learning every week from the beginning of your study schedule. This final prep period is for reviewing and taking timed exams.

> If you stretch the study schedule over several months, plan review weeks into your schedule. For example, every four weeks, use a few days to review the governing law and take timed exams. This is a practical and fruitful approach as you will be more likely to retain the information.

Pick specific dates for specific tasks; this makes it more likely you will complete them.

Make sure the tasks are measurable. (e.g., practice two MEE essays).

Be realistic about the tasks, time, energy, and your ability to complete the items listed as tasks in preparation for the exam.

Remember to take some scheduled breaks from studying.

Exercise, sleep and take care of your physical and mental health.

If you are not in the right mental state preparing for the exam, you will likely be ineffective when studying and are less likely to pass the exam.

Focused studying

Some people are better at multiple-choice questions; others do better with essays.

The multiple-choice portion (MBE at 50%) and the essay portion (MEE at 30% and MPT at 20%) are weighted equally.

Doing poorly in one section means it will be challenging to achieve a passing score.

Identify weaknesses early in the preparation process and focus on them.

If you struggle with multiple-choice questions, dedicate extra time to practicing MBE questions.

If you struggle with writing, focus on completing MEE essays and complete MPT practice materials.

By reviewing your performance on released multiple-choice practice tests, be concerned if you consistently miss questions that are most answered correctly.

If you have problems with questions and perform below 50%, you lack the fundamental knowledge necessary to pass the MBE.

When reviewing your answers to practice questions, it is essential to review all questions and answers, even those you got right.

Make sure you got that correct answer for the right reason.

Reviewing the questions and answers is critical for success on the exam.

Spend time reviewing those basic principles and working deliberately on the straightforward (and easy) questions that supplement learning.

Advice on using outlines

As a user of this governing law book, several of the following points are moot. They are included, so you can be confident that you are using the proper resources to prep for the bar.

Having a useful governing law study guide (such as this book) is critical.

Without effective resources, it is challenging to understand, learn and apply the governing law to the facts given in the question.

Some students use outlines that make learning difficult.

A few common mistakes about outlines:

- Learning outlines that are too long (e.g., more than 100 pages per subject) or too short (e.g., a seven-page Contracts outline). You will be overwhelmed by information or never learn enough governing law.

- Spending too much time comparing several outlines for the same subject.

  For example, using different Contracts outlines and needlessly comparing them. This confusion results in an undue focus on insignificant discrepancies.

- Outlining every subject. If you are not starting to study early, this consumes too much study time. Do not attempt to outline all subjects. It may be a good idea to outline a select few problematic subjects.

Using a detailed and well-organized governing law outline (e.g., this book) is essential; it saves time, organizes concepts, reduces anxiety, and helps you score well and pass the bar.

Easy questions make the difference

Limitations on the examiners lead to the first important insight into preparation for the exam – the kind of questions that decide whether you pass.

Performance on specific questions correlates with success or failure on the bar.

By analyzing statistics, questions predicting success or failure have been identified.

In general, the most challenging questions were not particularly good predictors of failure because most people who missed them passed the bar.

However, many of the straightforward questions were excellent predictors of success.

The median raw score ranges from about 60% to 66% correct on the MBE.

The National Conference of Bar Examiners (NCBE) writes, "expert panelists reported that they believed MBE items were generally easy, correctly estimating that about 66% of candidates would select the right answer to a typical item."

Depending on the exam's difficulty, in most states, scoring slightly below the median (miss up to 80 questions) still passes.

The most important questions to determine if you pass are not the exceedingly challenging ones but the easy ones where 90% of the examinees answer correctly.

The easy questions usually test a basic and regularly tested point of substantive law.

The wrong choices (i.e., the distracters) are typically easy to eliminate.

Your first task in preparing for the MBE is to get easy questions correct.

Study plan based upon statistics

These statistics show that an excellent performance on either the MBE questions (approximately 67% correct) or the state essays (4s on essays) assures you a passing score.

If you fail the MBE by 9 points or the essays by 5 points, the probability of passing the bar is in the single digits.

Put effort into performing well on the MBE questions for the following reasons.

- The questions are objective, and there are enough questions that are predictable concerning content and structure that it is possible, through reasonable effort, to answer 67% of the questions correctly.

- Studying the MBE first has the added advantage of preparing the necessary substantive law for state essays.

- The essays cover several subjects, the precise topic tested is unpredictable, and the answers are graded subjectively by graders who work quickly.

You had three years of law school practice with essays and less experience with multiple-choice questions.

Master the MBE before spending time preparing for the essays.

Factors associated with passing the bar

Based on an analysis of statistics from students' performance, the following factors predict the likelihood of passing the bar:

LSAT score

First-year Grade Point Average (GPA)

LSAT scores are a significant predictor of success on the bar because the LSAT requires similar multiple-choice test-taking skills as the MBE.

The LSAT tests many of the types of legal reasoning tested on the MBE.

A lower LSAT can be overcome by a comprehensive study of the MBE governing law, but these students must work harder.

Most of the subjects tested (e.g., constitutional law, civil procedure, contracts, criminal law, real property, torts) on the MBE are taken in the first year of law school.

First-year GPA measures mastery of subjects, preparedness for exams, and the ability to understand legal principles and apply them to given fact patterns.

The MBE measures the same factors but in a multiple-choice format instead of essays.

Pass rates based on GPA and LSAT scores

Past statistics indicate that law students with LSAT scores above 155 and a first-year GPA above 3.0 are reasonably assured of passing the bar.

They should study conscientiously and take practice MBEs to perform at the level needed, but they have little cause to panic.

Students with LSAT scores between 150 and 155 and a first-year GPA between 2.5 and 3.0 are in a bit more danger of failing and need to undertake rigorous preparation.

They must achieve a scaled score of 135 and take released practice exams and understand the reasons for incorrect choices. They should prepare for state essays by learning the governing laws in this book.

Students with LSAT scores between 145 and 150 and a first-year GPA between 2.2 and 2.5 have a moderate chance of passing the bar from deliberate efforts.

These students should not rely on ordinary commercial bar reviews and need intense training, particularly on the MBE component of the bar. They must devote 50-60 hours per week for seven weeks to prepare for the bar by learning the format and content of substantive law tested on the MBE. They should take released practice exams under exam conditions and conscientiously study the questions missed.

Students with LSAT scores below 145 and a GPA below 2.2 have had a failure rate of approximately 80%.

They must prep faithfully and conscientiously beyond the advice above and must engage in a rigorous course of study, more than is demanded by a traditional bar review course.

Notes for active learning

Learning and Applying the Substantive Law

Knowledge of substantive law

The fundamental reason for missing a question is 1) a failure to know the principle of law controlling the answer or 2) failure to understand how that principle is applied.

You must know and apply the governing law to pass the bar. If you do not know the governing law, you will not apply it to answer correctly.

Many students *think* they understand the governing law but do not know the nuances. Do not assume that you understand the governing (i.e., substantive) law. It is prevalent for students not to know the governing law well.

Re-learn the substantive and procedural law taught in first-year courses.

A major mistake is not to memorize the governing law outlined in this book.

The multiple-choice and essay portions test nuances and details of governing law. It is essential to analyze the governing law as it is applied in the context of the question.

On the multiple-choice section, many questions require fine-line distinctions between similar principles of law.

Several multiple-choice answers will *seem* correct, given the limited time to answer. If your knowledge of the governing law is suboptimal, you will not make these subtle distinctions and will have to guess on many questions.

For the essay to be developed, you must know the governing law and apply it to the issues within the call of the question.

If you do not know the governing law, you will not state the correct rule in your essay. You will be unable to apply the correct rule to the fact pattern.

Where to find the law

The questions must be related to the subject matter outlined in the bar examiners' (NCBE) materials.

While the NCBE outline is broad and ambiguous, years of experience with the exam delineate the scope of material you must learn.

The governing law covered in this book is foundational to the exam. The governing law statements were compiled by analyzing questions released by the multistate examiners. The analysis revealed a limited number of legal principles repeatedly tested.

Review these principles before taking practice exams and understand how they are applied to obtain the correct answer.

The property questions are probably the most difficult. The fact patterns are usually long and involve many parties in complex transactions.

In preparing for the exam, learn basic property principles and apply them. However, extensive studying into property law's crevices is not necessary to score well on these questions.

Feel confident that you do not have to go beyond the information provided in this book to find the governing law.

Controlling authority

The examiners have specified the sources of authority for the correct answers.

In Constitutional Law and Criminal Procedure, it is Supreme Court decisions.

In Criminal Law, it is common law.

In Evidence, the Federal Rules of Evidence controls.

In Torts and Property, it is the generally accepted view of United States law.

The UCC is the controlling authority in sales (Article 2) questions.

The NCBE released questions, and the published answers determine the controlling law through deduction.

Recent changes in the law

The exam is prepared months before it is given because of logistical requirements. Therefore, the examiners cannot incorporate recent changes in the law into the questions.

Recent changes in the law will not form the basis for correct answers.

If a recent change makes an answer initially designated as the correct answer to be incorrect, the examiners will credit more than one answer.

The recent holding of a Supreme Court case will not be tested for about two years since the decision was published.

Lesser-known issues and unusual applications

Some of the challenging exam questions are based on obscure principles of law.

Missing the most challenging questions will not cause you to fail the exam if you have a solid understanding of the governing law. You can learn these principles and answer the question correctly, thereby improving your overall performance.

There are instances where the correct answers are different from the usual rules.

For example, hearsay evidence inadmissible at trial is admissible before a judge hearing evidence on a preliminary question of fact (e.g., Federal Rules of Evidence 104(a)).

Practice applying the governing law

Some students know the governing law but have problems *applying* it to the facts.

The exam is as much about testing skills as it is about testing the governing law.

Therefore, knowledge of the governing law is not enough to pass.

You must practice answering multiple-choice questions and writing well-organized, coherent, and complete essays where you apply the governing law to the given facts.

Know which governing law is being tested

A typical wrong answer (i.e., distracter) on a question is an answer which is correct under a body of law other than the governing law being tested.

An example is a question governed by Article 2 of the Uniform Commercial Code (UCC), where an offer is irrevocable if:

1) it is in writing,

2) made by a merchant, and

3) states that it is irrevocable.

One of the wrong answers states the correct rule under the common law of contracts, where an offer is revocable unless consideration is paid (i.e., an option) for the promise to keep it open.

Answers which are always wrong

Some commonly used distracters are always wrong and can be eliminated quickly.

For example, a choice in an evidence question says, "character can only be attacked by reputation evidence." This choice is wrong because both opinion and reputation evidence is admissible under the Federal Rules of Evidence when character attacks are permissible.

Honing Reading Skills

Reading skills are critical. The basic level is reading to understand the facts, identify the issue and keep the parties distinct. A mistake at this juncture results in answering incorrectly, no matter how much law is known.

Understanding complex transactions

If the question involves a transaction with many parties, diagram the transaction before analyzing the choices.

The diagram should show the relationship between the parties (e.g., grantor-grantee, assignor-assignee), the transaction date, and the person's relationships in the transaction (e.g., donee, *bona fide* purchaser).

Impediments to careful reading

Two reasons candidates fail to read carefully are:

1) hurrying through a question,

2) fatigue due to a lack of sleep or strain caused by the exam.

A careful test taker maintains a steady, deliberate pace during the exam. Practice in advance and be well-rested on the test day.

Reading too much into a question

The examiners are committed to designing questions, which are "a fair index of whether the applicant has the ability to practice law." Psychometric experts ensure that they are fair and unbiased.

Even though you must read every word of these carefully drafted questions, do not read the question to find some bizarre interpretation.

The examiners must ask fair questions and not rely on "tricks." Reading too much into a question and looking for a trick lurking behind every fact leads to the wrong answer often.

It is the straightforward questions that determine whether you pass, not the occasional challenging question that tests some arcane principle of law.

Therefore, take questions at face value.

Read the call of the question first

Before reading the facts, read the call of the question because it indicates the task for selecting the correct answer. This perspective focuses your attention before reading the facts.

The question contains many *words of art*, such as "most likely," "best defense," or "least likely," which govern the correct answer.

The call is often phrased positively; the "best argument" or "most likely result."

Read answers for consistency with the question and eliminate inconsistent choices.

Negative calls

When the call of the question is negative, asking for the "weakest argument" or asking which of the options is "not" in a specified category, examine each option with the perspective that the choice with those negative characteristics is the correct answer.

After reading and understanding the question stem, read the call of the question again before reading the choices.

Analyze each choice with the requirements specified in the call of the question.

Read all choices

Never pick an answer until carefully reading all the choices. The objective is to pick the best answer, which cannot be determined until comparing the choices.

Sometimes the difference between the right and wrong answer is that one choice is more detailed or precisely sets forth the applicable law. You do not know that until reading all the answers carefully.

Broad statements of black letter law may be correct

When reading an answer, do not rule out choices with imprecise statements of the applicable *black letter* law.

If the examiners always included a choice that was precisely on point, the questions would be too easy. Instead, they often disguise the wording used in the correct answer.

For example, the Federal Rules of Evidence contain an elaborate set of relevancy rules that limit the right to introduce evidence of repairs after an accident. If there was a question where the introduction of that evidence was permissible, and no choices specifically cite the exception to the general rule of exclusion, an answer phrased with the general rule of relevancy "Admissible because its probative value outweighs its prejudicial effect," would be the correct answer.

Multiple-Choice Test-Taking Tactics

Determine the single correct answer

Increase the odds of picking the correct answer based on technical factors independent of substantive (governing) law knowledge.

The examiners' limitation is that every question must have one demonstrably correct and three demonstrably incorrect answers, limiting how the examiners write the choices.

From the question's construction, this limitation may give clues about the answer.

Process of elimination

Answering a multiple-choice question is not finding the ideal answer to the question asked but instead picking the best option.

Eliminate choices and evaluate the remaining choice for plausibility.

Eliminate choices that state an incorrect proposition of law or do not relate to the facts.

If you eliminate three options and the remaining one is acceptable, pick it and move on.

Elimination increases the odds

It takes about 125 correct answers to pass the MBE. An important strategy in reaching that number is intelligently eliminating choices.

If you are sure of the answer to only 50 of the 200 questions on the exam and confidently eliminate two of the four choices on the remaining 150 questions. Guess between the two remaining choices, and the odds predict 75 correct.

Those 75 correct, coupled with 50 questions you were confident of the answer, produce a raw score of 125 on the MBE and a scaled score above the benchmark 135.

Unfortunately, you cannot avoid guessing on questions, but intelligent methods reduce options to only two viable choices.

Sometimes you might not be able to eliminate the wrong answers just because you are sure of the answer to one of the choices. Eliminating with confidence even one choice increases the probability of correctly answering the question.

Eliminating two wrong answers

Specific questions on the MBE are challenging because of distinguishing between two choices when selecting the best answer.

A typical comment from examinees leaving the exam is, "I could not decide between the last two choices."

The positive side of that problem is eliminating two of the four choices.

Pick the winning side

The most common choice pattern is the "two-two" pattern – two choices state that the plaintiff prevails, and two that the defendant prevails.

The best approach for this type of question is to rely on your knowledge of the law or instinctive feeling to which conclusion is correct.

In a question with two choices on one side and two on the other side of a court's decision, first, pick a choice on the side you think should prevail.

Distinguish between the explanations following this conclusion and pick the choice that best justifies it.

Distance between choices on the other side

If the justifications following the conclusion for the side you chose seem indistinguishable, look at the explanations for the choices on the other side.

If the reasons for the choices on the other side are readily distinguishable, and one appears reasonable and the other incorrect, reconsider your initial conclusion.

Remember, the examiner is required to provide a distinguishable reason why one explanation of a general conclusion is correct, and the other is wrong.

That obligation does not exist if the general conclusion itself is incorrect.

Suppose choices (A) and (B) on one side look correct; that is, they are reasonable and consistent with the fact pattern. One of the choices with the opposite conclusion, answer (C), seems incorrect or inconsistent with the facts, and answer (D) with the same general conclusion sounds reasonable. From a strictly technical viewpoint, the best choice is answer (D).

Questions based upon a common fact pattern

There are several instances where two or more questions are based on the same facts.

Look at the second question's wording to guide the first question's correct answer. When asked to assume an answer to a first question from a fact pattern to answer the second question, the probability is high that the answer to the first question follows that assumption.

For example, if the first question has two choices beginning with "P prevails" and two with "D prevails," and the second question starts with "If P prevails," it is likely one of the "P prevails" choices is correct for the first question. If you picked "D prevails," think carefully before selecting it as the final answer.

Multiple true/false issues

In addition to true/false questions, the exam sometimes states three propositions in the root of the question and tests characteristics of those propositions in the call of the question.

The choices list various combinations of propositions.

The difference between this type of question and the double true/false question is that only four of the eight possible combinations fit into the options. It is possible to answer correctly even if you are not sure of all propositions' truth or falsity but are sure of one.

Correctly stated, but the inapplicable principle of law

The task of the examiners is to make the wrong choices look attractive. A creative way to accomplish this is to write a choice that impeccably states a rule of law that is not applicable because of facts in the root of the question.

For example, in a question where a person is an assignee, not a sublessee, one of the choices may correctly state the law for sublessees, but it is inapplicable to the fact pattern.

Therefore, these answer choices with inapplicable law can be confidently eliminated.

"Because" questions

Conjunctions are commonly used in the answers. It is essential to understand their role in determining whether a choice is correct.

The word "because" connects a conclusion and the reason for that conclusion with the facts in the body of the question.

There are two requirements for a question using "because" to be correct:

1) the conclusion must be correct,

2) the reasoning must logically follow based upon facts in the question, and the statement which follows "because" must be legally correct.

If the "because" choice has the correct result for the wrong reason, it is incorrect.

"If" questions

The conjunction "if" requires a much narrower focus than "because."

When a choice contains an "if," determine whether the entire statement is true, assuming that the proposition which follows the "if" is true.

There is no requirement that facts in the root of the question support the proposition following "if." There is no requirement for facts in the question to support the proposition that such a construction be reasonable.

"Because" or "if" need not be exclusive

There is no requirement for the conclusion following "if" or "because" to be exclusive.

For example, if a master could be liable in tort under the doctrine of *respondeat superior* or because the master was *negligent*, a choice using "if" or "because" holding the master liable would be correct if it stated either reason, even though the master might be liable for the other reason.

Exam tip for "because"

Notice that in an answer that would have been correct, the word "because" limits the facts you could consider to those in the body of the question containing specific facts.

The difference between the effect of "if" and "because" controls the answer.

Identify those limited situations (e.g., where the appropriate standard is strict liability) and distinguish them from those that are satisfactory (e.g., if the standard is negligence).

"Only if" requires exclusivity

Sometimes the words "only if" are used to distinguish between the two "affirmed" choices to make one wrong.

When an option uses the words "only if," assume that the entire proposition is correct as long as the words following "only if" are true.

The critical difference, where "only if" is used, is that the proposition cannot be true except when the condition is true. If there is another reason for the same result to be reached, the choice is wrong.

"Unless" questions

The conjunction "unless" has the same function as "only if," except that it precedes a negative exclusive condition instead of a positive exclusive condition.

It is essentially the mirror image of an "only if" choice.

For an option using "unless," reverse and substitute the words "only if" for "unless."

Limiting words

Choices can be made incorrect with limiting words that require that a proposition be true in all circumstances or under no circumstances.

Examples of limiting words include *all*, *any*, *never*, *always*, *only*, *every*, and *plenary*.

Notes for active learning

Making Correct Judgment Calls

Applying the law to the facts

Most questions give a fact pattern and ask which choice draws the correct legal conclusion required by the call of the question.

The first skill required is to draw inferences from facts given to place the conduct described in the question in the appropriate legal category.

The second skill is to apply the appropriate legal rule to conduct in that category and choose the option which reaches the appropriate conclusion.

The process of drawing inferences from a fact pattern and placing conduct in an appropriate category often requires judgment.

Bad judgment equals the wrong answer

To make the questions difficult, the examiners often place the conduct near the border of two different legal classifications.

Decide which side of the demarcation the conduct falls on. Inevitably, reasonable people can differ on these judgments.

If your judgment does not match the examiners, you will likely answer the question incorrectly, no matter how much law you know.

Mitigate this problem by reviewing released questions involving judgment calls where the examiners have published correct answers (i.e., their judgment call).

For example, a death occurring because the parties played Russian roulette is considered *depraved heart murder*, not *involuntary manslaughter*.

Judgment calls happen

Difficult judgment calls occur several times on the exam, and you are likely to make some close judgment calls incorrectly.

While this adds to the frustrations of multiple-choice tests, it is part of the exam.

By narrowing judgment call questions to two choices and guessing, you will get approximately half of them correct.

You will not fail the exam solely because you were unlucky on judgment calls.

The examiners remove many judgment calls by procedural devices.

The importance of procedure

The question may not ask what a jury should find on the facts.

The answer may be controlled by the procedural context of the criminal prosecution.

For example, it is given that the jury has found the defendant guilty of murder, and the only question on appeal is whether the judge should have granted a motion to dismiss at the end of hearing evidence. This is because a reasonable jury looking at the facts and inferences most favorable to the prosecution should not have found the defendant guilty of murder.

The same procedural issues exist when the question asks if a motion for summary judgment should be allowed or if the court should direct a verdict.

Exam Tips and Suggestions

Timing is everything

The time given to complete the exam is usually adequate if you practiced enough questions to improve speed and efficiency to the required level.

As you get closer to the test date, just doing practice questions is not enough.

You need to time your practice. Take previously released exams in two three-hour periods on the same day. Since these practice exams are approximately the same length as the exam, you will know if you have a timing problem.

If you do not practice under timed conditions, you risk exhausting time on the exam before answering all the questions.

Practice your timing under test-like conditions to know if the timing will be an issue. If you cannot complete the practice exam, you will have trouble with the exam.

If time is an issue, adjust your pace and continue practicing.

All questions do not require the same amount of time.

An approach for when time is not an issue

If you can complete 100 questions in three hours, use this strategy. At the start of the exam, break the allotted time into 15-minute intervals and write them down.

Set an initial pace of 9 questions every fifteen minutes.

Check your progress at each 15-minute interval.

If you completed 18 questions in the first half-hour, 36 in the first hour, 72 in the first two hours, and 90 in the first two and a half hours, you are on target to complete the exam on time. At this pace, you should complete 100 questions in two hours and forty-six minutes.

This leaves 14 minutes to check the answer sheet, revisit troublesome questions, or use the time to go a little slower on the last questions when fatigue impairs acuity.

If you find that your careful pace is faster than the budgeted 9 questions every 15 minutes, work at a faster pace, but use the extra time on the more challenging questions or in rechecking your work at the end.

Do *not* change the original answer choice unless you have a specific reason.

It is unwise to leave the exam early.

An approach for when time is an issue

During practice, continue answering questions to complete the section even after the time for self-paced exams has expired. Note which question you completed within the allocated time. Strive to complete the questions within the allotted time during your final exam prep.

If you learn from taking the practice test that you may not finish the questions in the allotted time on the actual exam, skip those questions with a long fact pattern followed by only one question. Keep your place on the answer sheet by skipping the row.

Return to those questions at the end and complete as many as time permits. Before turning your exam in, guess at the rest to reduce the number of random guesses.

Answer every question, even if you have not read the question, since wrong answers do *not* count against you.

Difficult questions

If you do not know the answer, do not spend a disproportionate amount of time on it since each question counts the same. Mark it in the test booklet, make a shrewd guess within the budgeted time and come back if time allows.

Do *not* leave questions unanswered. No points are deducted for wrong answers.

Minimize fatigue to maximize your score

The mental energy required to answer all the multiple-choice questions under stress produces fatigue (even with a lunch break).

Fatigue slows processing questions effectively and impairs reading comprehension. You may process questions more slowly at the end of each session and more quickly at the beginning before fatigue sets in.

Take at least two released exams under timed conditions to know how significantly fatigue affects your performance.

Be sure to arrive at the exam site on time. If necessary, stay at a nearby hotel rather than getting up early and risking a long drive the morning of the exam.

Relax during the lunch break and do not discuss the morning session with others.

You should know enough about your metabolism to eat the correct foods during the exam and reinforce appropriate caffeine levels if appropriate.

Proofread the answer sheet

As you decide on each correct answer, circle the corresponding letter in the exam book, and mark the appropriate block on the answer sheet.

The answer sheet is the only document graded by the examiners.

At the pace of 9 questions per 15 minutes, about 14 minutes should remain. Spend that time proofreading the answer sheet. Verify the answers circled to be certain that you marked the appropriate block on the answers.

Ensure that there are no blanks, and no questions have two answers.

Do *not* use this time to change an answer already selected unless you have a particularly good reason to change it.

If you have erased, ensure the erasure is thorough, or the computer may reject the answer because it cannot distinguish between marked answers.

If you have time after proofreading, review the problematic questions, and re-think the answers chosen. However, even after careful thought, hesitate to change an answer.

Do not leave any section of the exam early; use the allotted time wisely.

Intelligent preparation over a sustained period

There is no easy way to conquer an exam as challenging and comprehensive as the MBE, except through practice and an investment of time and effort well before the exam.

By diligently preparing, practicing questions, and intelligently assessing why questions were answered incorrectly, your skills for the exam will improve substantially.

Continue to improve those skills by following the advice given herein until reaching a proficiency level enabling you to pass the bar. This proficiency is accurately measured in multiple-choice format questions.

Some students will have to work harder to achieve the required proficiency.

The tools are in this study guide, and any law school graduate can be successful in passing the bar if they invest the required time and effort to be prepared.

Notes for active learning

Essay Preparation Strategies and Essay-Writing Suggestions

Memorize the law

Do not make the mistake of waiting too long before memorizing the governing law. Start learning the governing law early to be better prepared and pass the exam.

Memorize essential principles and focus on highly tested governing law.

Focus on the highly tested essay rules

Do not treat all subjects the same when you prepare for the essay portion of the exam.

Some governing law topics are tested more than others. It is crucial to focus on the highly tested topics (e.g., torts, contracts. property, civil procedure).

Know and apply enough governing laws to pass the bar – focus on commonly tested governing laws (e.g., negligence) provided in this book.

Practice writing essay answers each week

Practicing is crucial to a high score on essays. Practice regularly and avoid procrastination for this essential component of bar prep.

Incorporate practicing essay writing into your exam study schedule. To reduce procrastination, schedule time for writing practice essays each week.

For the MPT, practice by drafting full MPTs. Most examinees procrastinate on preparing for the MPT; there is nothing to memorize.

Do not make the *fatal mistake* of not practicing. The MPT portion is worth 20% of the UBE score.

Know the format and *practice that format to* increase your UBE score. This practice will increase your score and the probability of passing the bar.

Add one essay-specific subject each week

The Multistate Essay Exam (MEE) subjects include the 7 MBE subjects plus the 5 subjects of Business Associations (Agency, Partnerships, Corporations, and LLCs), Conflict of Laws, Family Law, Trusts and Estates, and Secured Transactions (UCC Article 9).

Combine highly tested subjects (e.g., torts) with less-tested subjects (e.g., secured transactions) and complex topics (e.g., contracts) with easier topics (e.g., business associations).

From preparation, know which subjects you struggle with and require a focused effort to master the essential governing law.

Make it easy for the grader to award points

Your answer to a question will probably be read in less than five minutes by a grader with a checklist to find that you have seen the issues and discussed them intelligently. Writing organized and clear answers makes it easy for the essay grader to award points.

Use headings for each of the major issues.

If the question suggests a structure for the answer because it is divided into parts or because the facts present a series of discrete issues, use the structure of the question, which is probably the structure of the checklist.

Use the IRAC method for the essay questions: state the issue, state the Rule. Apply the rule to the facts and conclude. IRAC seems simple, but following this approach makes it easier for the grader to know that you identified and addressed every issue and applied the law to the facts given.

IRAC results in more points during the exam.

Do not spend time trying to formulate eloquent issue statements. The question often outlines the issues, so an eloquent issue statement is redundant, and issue statements do not earn extra points.

Many examinees spend too much time developing an impressive issue statement and omit other essentials of their analysis (e.g., truncated analysis section).

An issue statement "Torts" or "Is the defendant liable for negligence?" is enough.

Do not waste time arguing both sides. There are no "two sides" for many essays to argue on bar essays because these are not law school essays.

Apply the law to facts and conclude unless asserting each party has good arguments.

Conclusion for each essay question

Points will be lost unless you conclude for each issue identified in the facts or are asked to address it in the call of the question.

Use caution starting the essay with the conclusion unless confident it is correct.

Many sample answers provided by the National Conference of Bar Examiners start with a definite and strong conclusion. Use caution to start with a conclusion unless confident (e.g., NCBE sample responses) your conclusion is correct.

Starting with a conclusion that is not correct draws attention to an incorrect conclusion at the start, which may influence the grader disproportionality. The grader may lose faith in your answer from the onset, and it is advisable to have a neutral heading rather than a firm conclusion that is wrong.

Tips for an easy-to-read essay

Use paragraph breaks between the Issue, Rule, Analysis, and Conclusion. Paragraph break makes it easy for the grader to read and score your essays. Additionally, this approach makes the answer appear longer and more complete.

Emphasize keywords and phrases. Underline key phrases so the grader notices that you addressed the governing law and applied it to the facts given.

After graders score several essays on the same topic, they scan essays for specific phrases that they expect to locate within a complete essay.

Think before you write

Read each question carefully to understand the facts and their necessary implications thoroughly and accurately.

After skimming the question, spend time on the focus line at the end of the question. Review the facts with the call of the question in mental focus.

Write a short outline of the issues raised. Outline in your mind the issues; state to yourself the tentative conclusions; test each conclusion from the standpoints of law and common sense; revise, as necessary.

Decide on a logical, orderly, and convincing arrangement for the response. Until then, you are not ready to write the answer.

Of the thirty-six minutes allotted to each essay, spend 15 minutes on issue spotting and organization and about twenty minutes writing the answer.

The ability to think and communicate like a lawyer

The Board knows that you have completed law school, under competent instructors, and have passed law school exams. The bar does not challenge the results of your law school courses.

The exam tests the ability to apply what you have learned to facts that might arise in practice and which, in some instances, involve several fields of law. The value of an answer depends not only on the correctness of the conclusions but on displaying essential legal principles and thinking like a lawyer.

Conclude on each issue presented. If a conclusion is derived from fuzzy facts, construct a well-reasoned argument supporting your conclusion to receive full credit regardless of if you conclude the same as the examiners.

If the correct answer depends on a provision of substantive law, which you are not familiar with, you can obtain a passing answer to the question by reaching a well-reasoned conclusion applying general law principles.

Do not try to limit the question to a particular subject area. Many questions combine traditional subjects, and you must be prepared to answer the question applying principles you learned across various subjects.

Do not restate the facts

The examiners know the facts; there is no time to waste. Do not restate the facts but use them to apply and integrate legal principles in writing the essay.

Do not fight the facts, particularly the focus line of the question.

For example, if the facts state that A executed a valid will, write about valid wills. If the question asks you to argue on behalf of A, do not argue on behalf of B because B has a prevailing argument. However, raise potential arguments which could be made on behalf of B and counter them in arguing on behalf of A.

Do not state abstract or irrelevant propositions of law

It is usually undesirable to begin an answer with a legal proposition. If the proposition is applicable, it will be more appropriate later to indicate the reason for your conclusion. If it is not applicable, do not state a surplus fact or legal principle.

Although it is seldom necessary to state an applicable rule of law in detail, make a sufficient reference to it so that the examiner appreciates your knowledge of the principle and conditions when it applies.

Do not, by speculating on different facts, nor in other ways, work into your answer some point of law with which you happen to be familiar, but which does not apply to the answer. Importantly, the examiners are not interested in knowing how many rules of law you know, but your ability to apply the applicable rules to the facts.

If the question says that A and B in the above hypothetical are unrelated, do not talk about the results which would occur if they were husband and wife.

Use the principles of law applicable to the call of the question and the facts. You must state the principles of applicable law to demonstrate to the examiner that you know the elements of the rule and how they apply to these facts.

For example, if the facts said that A transferred to B (a non-relative) the money necessary for B to purchase Blackacre from C and asks who owns Blackacre, you would say, "Since A furnished the consideration for the purchase of Blackacre and B took the title to the property in their name, B holds title to Blackacre in a resulting trust for A.

Do not detail the black letter law of resulting trusts since you have shown your knowledge by properly applying the facts to the law of resulting trusts.

Do not fight the facts and address a contrary fact not presented. The examiners may take points away if you make that mistake because you are not focused on the issues presented.

Discuss all the issues raised

A grasp of all the issues is essential.

For example, if there are three issues in a question, a discussion of only one issue, no matter how masterly, if coupled with omitting the others, could not result in 100% credit. It would probably result in a score of 33%.

The exam includes many issues in most questions so it can be graded mechanically. This maintains consistency across a group of several graders for each exam question.

The grader has a checklist of issues and awards most points for the examinee that identifies issues and intelligently discusses each.

Failure to see and discuss enough issues intelligently is probably the biggest reason for failure on the essay portion of the exam.

Methods for finding all issues

Use all the facts presented. Failure to discuss facts probably means that you missed important issues.

If you must decide in the early part of the question (e.g., does the court have jurisdiction) and you decide that issue so the remaining facts become irrelevant, make an alternative assumption ("If the court does have jurisdiction") and answer the question in the alternative using facts which would otherwise be irrelevant.

Do not avoid issues because you are not sure of the substantive law. If the examiners stated that X's nephew helped X escape after a crime, discuss the nephew's status as an accessory after the fact. If you do not know whether he is a close enough relative to be exempt under the statute, answer this issue by making alternative assumptions.

Indicators requiring alternative arguments

Ambiguous terms – if there are words in the fact pattern that are neutral or ambiguous such as "put up," the examiners look for possible interpretations of these terms.

Language in quotes – language placed in quotes is almost always ambiguous and must be construed as part of the answer.

Avoid ambiguous, rambling statements and verbosity

Generally, do not use compound sentences. Two separate sentences are preferred.

Complex sentences are particularly useful to apply the facts of the question to the applicable principle of law.

For example, in the previous resulting trust hypothetical, write, "Since B purchased Blackacre and took title in their name with money furnished by A, A holds title to Blackacre in a resulting trust, even if B has not signed a memorandum."

Avoid undue repetition

If the same principle of law and conclusion apply to two parts of an answer, state it once in detail, and refer back for the second part.

For example, if you have discussed A's liability and now must discuss B's liability, say, "B is also guilty of murder for the same reasons as A. (see discussion above)."

Avoid slang and colloquialism

The examiners judge your formal writing style.

If the examiner shows humor with names and events, do not show your sense of humor.

Use the standard abbreviations:

P for Plaintiff

D for Defendant

K for Contract

BFP for *Bona Fide* purchaser

Write legibly and coherently

Printing is usually easier to read than handwriting.

Use all the pages, and do not crowd your answer.

Plan your answer so that you do not have to use inserts and arrows.

Timing strategies

On the MEE, you must complete six equally weighted essay questions in three hours; an average of 30 minutes per question.

You have flexibility with time limitations as questions are not of the same difficulty.

There are two absolute figures:

>spend no more than 45 minutes on any question,

>spend at least 20 minutes on each question.

Be careful about not going over the time limit on the first question because this will require a readjustment of your timing for the entire session. If you miss the deadlines, re-divide your remaining time so that you will have an equal amount of time on each question.

If you go over by 15 minutes a question, do not allocate 30 minutes for other questions.

Stay focused

Do not start by reading the entire exam. Answer the questions in order and do not consider more than one question at a time.

After answering, put it out of your mind and not worry about your response. Keep your mind clear to focus on the next question.

Proofread your answers as time permits.

Law school essay grading matrix

An "A" answer is an outstanding response. It correctly and fully identifies dispositive issues and sub-issues raised by the question. The answer states the applicable legal rules and sub-rules with precision. It analyzes the question thoroughly with the applicable rules and explores alternative analysis where appropriate. It applies the law to the facts to conclude and is not cluttered by irrelevant matters. An "A" answer demonstrates an objectively superior mastering of the subject. An answer is not an "A" answer simply because it is better than most students' answers.

A "B" answer is a good response. It presents the four components of a good answer (issues, rules, analysis & application, and conclusion), but it does so in a way that could be improved. For example, it may be that not all critical issues have been spotted, or the issues are not presented clearly. The statement of legal rules captures that basic law but may not develop the law's complexities or nuances. The analysis is competent but lacks subtlety and may be somewhat simplistic or conclusory.

A "C" answer is a minimally competent response. It contains the four components of a good answer (issues, rules, analysis & application, and conclusion) but may not distinguish them. Perhaps only some issues have been identified while others are missed. The rules of law lack completeness or accuracy. The analysis and application may be shallow and conclusory. Conclusions may be questionable and not well-defended.

A "D" answer lacks basic components. It may identify the wrong issues or none. Rules are stated incorrectly. The analysis is conclusory or absent. The law is not applied to the facts coherently. Conclusions are unsupported or missing. The response exhibits a lack of knowledge of legal issues and rules or demonstrates an inability to engage in legal analysis.

Best wishes with your preparation!

Appendix

Overview of American Law

Overview of American Law

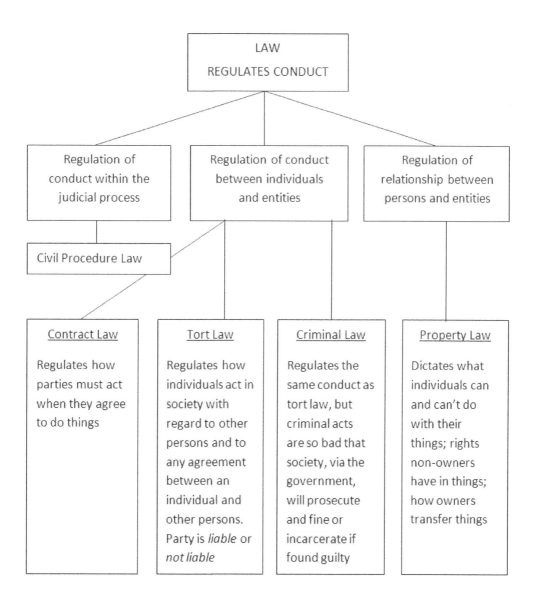

U.S. Court Systems – Federal and State Courts

There are two kinds of courts in the USA – federal courts and state courts.

Federal courts are established under the U.S. Constitution by Congress to decide disputes involving the Constitution and laws passed by Congress. A state establishes state and local courts (within states, local courts are established by cities, counties, and other municipalities).

Jurisdiction of federal and state courts

The differences between federal courts and state courts are defined by jurisdiction.[1] Jurisdiction refers to the kinds of cases that a particular court is authorized to hear and adjudicate (i.e., the pronouncement of a legally binding judgment upon the parties to the dispute).

Federal court jurisdiction is limited to the types of cases listed in the Constitution and specifically provided by Congress. For the most part, federal courts only hear:

- cases in which the United States is a party[2];

- cases involving violations of the U.S. Constitution or federal laws (under federal-question jurisdiction[3]);

- cases between citizens of different states if the amount in controversy *exceeds* $75,000 (under diversity jurisdiction[4]); and

- bankruptcy, copyright, patent, and maritime law cases.

State courts, in contrast, have broad jurisdiction, so the cases individual citizens are likely to be involved in (e.g., robberies, traffic violations, contracts, and family disputes) are usually heard and decided in state courts. The only cases state courts are not allowed to hear are lawsuits against the United States and those involving certain specific federal laws: criminal, antitrust, bankruptcy, patent, copyright, and some maritime law cases.

In many cases, both federal and state courts have jurisdiction whereby the plaintiff (i.e., the party initiating the suit) can choose whether to file their claim in state or federal court.

Criminal cases involving federal laws can be tried only in federal court, but most criminal cases involve violations of state law and are tried in state court. Robbery is a crime, but what law makes it is a crime? Except for certain exceptions, state laws, not federal laws, make robbery a crime. There are only a few federal laws about robbery, such as the law that makes it a federal crime to rob a bank whose deposits are insured by a federal agency. Examples of other federal crimes are the transport of illegal drugs into the country or across state lines and using the U.S. mail system to defraud consumers.

Crimes committed on federal property (e.g., national parks or military reservations) are prosecuted in federal court.

Federal courts may hear cases concerning state laws if the issue is whether the state law violates the federal Constitution. Suppose a state law forbids slaughtering animals outside of certain limited areas. A neighborhood association brings a case in state court against a defendant who sacrifices chickens in their backyard. When the court issues an order (i.e., an injunction[5]) forbidding the defendant from further sacrifices, the defendant challenges the state law in federal court as an unconstitutional infringement of religious freedom.

Some conduct is illegal under both federal and state laws. For example, federal laws prohibit employment discrimination, and the states have added additional legal restrictions. A person can file their claim in either federal or state court under federal law or federal and state laws. A case that only involves a state law can be brought only in state court.

Appeals for review of actions by federal administrative agencies are federal civil cases.

For example, if the Environmental Protection Agency, over the objection of area residents, issued a permit to a paper mill to discharge water used in its milling process into the Scenic River, the residents may appeal and have the federal court of appeals review the agency's decision.

---

[1] *jurisdiction* – 1) the legal authority of a court to hear and decide specific types of case; 2) the geographic area over which the court has the authority to decide cases.

[2] *parties* – the plaintiff and the defendant in a lawsuit.

[3] *federal-question jurisdiction* – the federal district courts' authorization to hear and decide cases arising under the Constitution, laws, or treaties of the United States.

[4] *diversity jurisdiction* – the federal district courts' authority to hear and decide civil cases involving plaintiffs and defendants who are citizens of different states (or U.S. citizens and foreign nationals) and meet specific statutory requirements.

[5] *injunction* – a judge's order that a party takes or refrain from taking a particular action. An injunction may be preliminary until the outcome of a case is determined or permanent.

Organization of the federal courts

Congress has divided the country into 94 federal judicial districts, with each having a U.S. district court. The U.S. district courts are the federal trial courts -- where federal cases are tried, witnesses testify, and juries serve.

Each district has a U.S. bankruptcy court, which is part of the district court that administers the U.S. bankruptcy laws.

Congress uses state boundaries to help define the districts. Some districts cover an entire state, like Idaho. Other districts cover just part of a state, like the Northern District of California. Congress placed each of the ninety-four districts in one of twelve regional circuits whereby each circuit has a court of appeals. The losing party can petition the court of appeals to review the case to determine if the district judge applied the law correctly.

There is a U.S. Court of Appeals for the Federal Circuit, whose jurisdiction is defined by subject matter rather than geography. It hears appeals from certain courts and agencies, such as the U.S. Court of International Trade, the U.S. Court of Federal Claims, and the U.S. Patent and Trademark Office, and certain types of cases from the district courts (mainly lawsuits claiming that patents have been infringed).

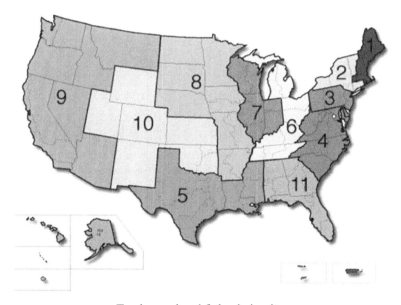

Twelve regional federal circuits

The Supreme Court in Washington, D.C., is the highest court in the nation. The losing party can petition in a case in the court of appeals (or, sometimes, in a state supreme court), can petition the Supreme Court to hear an appeal.

Unlike a court of appeals, the Supreme Court does not have to hear the case. The Supreme Court hears only a small percentage of the cases it is asked to review.

Notes for active learning

How Civil Cases Move Through the Federal Courts

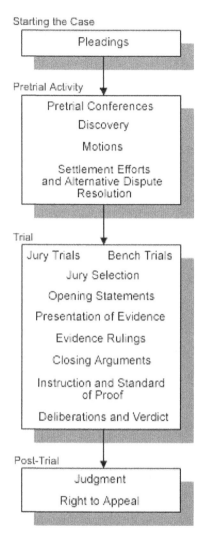

A federal civil case begins when a person, or their legal representative, files a paper with the clerk of the court that asserts another person's wrongful act injured the person. In legal terminology, the plaintiff files a *complaint* against the defendant.

The defendant files an *answer* to the complaint. These written statements of the party's positions are called pleadings. In some circumstances, the defendant may file a *motion* instead of an answer; the motion asks the court to take some action, such as dismiss the case or require the plaintiff to explain more clearly what the lawsuit is about.

Jury trials

In a jury trial, the jury decides what happened, and to apply the legal standards, the judge tells them to apply to reach a verdict. The plaintiff presents evidence supporting its view of the case, and the defendant presents evidence rebutting the plaintiff's evidence or supporting its view of the case. From these presentations, the jury must decide what happened and applied the law to those facts.

The jury never decides what law applies to the case; that is the role of the judge. For example, in a discrimination case where the plaintiff alleged that their workplace was hostile, the judge tells the jury the legal standard for a hostile environment.

The jury would have to decide whether the plaintiff's description of events was true and whether those events met the legal standard. A trial jury, or petit jury, may consist of six to twelve jurors in a civil case.

151

Bench trials

If the parties agree not to have a *jury trial* and leave the fact-finding to the judge, the trial is a *bench trial*. In bench and jury trials, the judge ensures the correct legal standards are followed.

In contrast to a jury trial, the judge decides the facts and renders the verdict in a *bench trial*.

For example, in a discrimination case in which the plaintiff alleged a hostile environment, the judge would determine the legal standard for a hostile environment and decide whether the plaintiff's description of events was true and whether those events met the legal standard.

Some kinds of cases always have bench trials. For example, there is never a jury trial if the plaintiff is seeking an injunction, an order from the judge that the defendant does, or stop doing something, as opposed to monetary damages.

Some statutes provide that a judge must decide the facts in certain types of cases.

Jury selection

A jury trial begins with the selection of jurors. Citizens are selected for jury service through a process set out in laws passed by Congress and in the federal rules of procedure.

First, citizens are called to court to be available to serve on juries. These citizens are selected at random from sources, in most districts, lists of registered voters, which may be augmented by other sources, such as lists of licensed drivers in the judicial district.

The judge and the lawyers choose who will serve on the jury.

To choose the jurors, the judge and sometimes the lawyers ask prospective jurors questions to determine if they will decide the case fairly, a process known as *voir dire*.

The lawyers may request that the judge excuse jurors they think may not be impartial, such as those who know a party in the case or who have had an experience that might make them favor one side over the other. These requests for rejecting jurors are *challenges for cause*.

The lawyers may request that the judge excuse a certain number of jurors without reason; these requests are *peremptory challenges*.

Instructions and standard of proof

Following the closing arguments, the judge gives instructions to the jury, explaining the relevant law, how the law applies to the case, and what questions the jury must decide.

How sure do jurors have to be before they reach a verdict? One important instruction the judge gives the jury is the standard of proof they must follow in deciding the case.

The courts, through their decisions, and Congress, through statutes, have established standards by which facts must be proven in criminal and civil cases.

In civil cases, to decide for the plaintiff, the jury must determine by a *preponderance of the evidence* that the defendant failed to perform a legal duty and violated the plaintiff's rights. A preponderance of the evidence means that, based on the evidence, the evidence favors the plaintiff more (even if only slightly) than it favors the defendant.

If the evidence in favor of the plaintiff could be placed on one side of a scale and that in favor of the defendant on the other, the plaintiff would win if the evidence in favor of the plaintiff was heavy enough to tip the scale. If the two sides were even, or if the scale tipped for the defendant, the defendant would win.

Judgment

In civil cases, if the jury (or judge) decides in favor of the plaintiff, the result usually is that the defendant must pay the plaintiff money or damages. The judge orders the defendant to pay the decided amount. Sometimes the defendant is ordered to take some specific action that will restore the plaintiff's rights. If the defendant wins the case, there is nothing more the trial court needs to do as the case is disposed of and the defendant is held not liable.

Right to appeal

The losing party in a federal civil case has a right to appeal the verdict to the U.S. court of appeals (i.e., Federal Circuit Courts) and ask the court to review the case to determine whether the trial was conducted properly. The losing party in the state trial court has a right to appeal the verdict to the state court of appeal.

The grounds for appeal usually are that the federal district (or state) judge made an error, either in the procedure (e.g., admitting improper evidence) or interpreting the law. The government may appeal in civil cases, as any other party may. Neither party may appeal if there was no trial -- parties settled their civil case out of court.

Notes for active learning

How Criminal Cases Move Through the Federal Courts

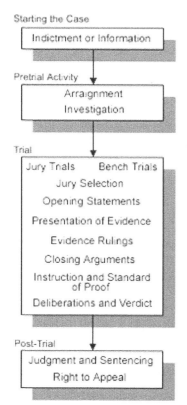

Indictment or information

A criminal case formally begins with an indictment or information, which is a formal accusation that a person committed a crime.

An indictment may be obtained when a lawyer (i.e., prosecutor) for the executive branch of the U.S. government (i.e., U.S. attorney or assistant U.S. attorney) present evidence to a federal grand jury that, according to the government, indicates a person committed a crime.

The U.S. attorney tries to convince the grand jury that there is enough evidence to show that the person probably committed the crime and should be formally accused. If the grand jury agrees, it issues an indictment.

A grand jury is different from a trial jury or petit jury.

A grand jury determines whether the person may be tried for a crime; a petit jury listens to the evidence presented at the trial and determines whether the defendant is guilty.

Petit is French for "small"; petit juries usually consist of twelve jurors in criminal cases.

Grand is French for "large"; grand juries have from sixteen to twenty-three jurors.

Grand jury indictments are most often used for *felonies* (i.e., punishable by imprisonment of more than a year or by death) such as bank robberies or sales of illegal drugs.

Grand jury indictments are not necessary to prosecute *misdemeanors* (i.e., less serious than a felony but more serious than an infraction) and are necessary for felonies.

For lesser crimes, the U.S. attorney issues an *information* that substitutes for an indictment. For example, speeding on a highway in a national park is a misdemeanor.

An information is used when a defendant waives an indictment by a grand jury.

Arraignment

After the grand jury issues the indictment, the accused (i.e., defendant) is summoned to court or arrested (if not already in custody). The next step is an arraignment, a proceeding in which the defendant is brought before a judge, told of the charges they are accused of, and asked to plead guilty or not guilty. If the defendant's plea is guilty, a time is set for the defendant to return to court to be sentenced.

If the defendant pleads "not guilty," the time is set for the trial.

A defendant may enter a plea bargain with the prosecution--usually by agreeing to plead guilty to some but not all charges or lesser charges. The prosecution drops the remaining charges.

About nine out of ten defendants in criminal cases plead guilty.

Investigation

In a criminal case, a defense lawyer conducts a thorough investigation before trial, interviewing witnesses, visiting the crime scene, and examining physical evidence. An important part of this investigation is determining whether the evidence the government plans to use to prove its case was obtained legally.

The Fourth Amendment to the Constitution forbids unreasonable searches and seizures. To enforce this protection, the Supreme Court has decided that illegally seized evidence cannot be used at trial for most purposes.

For example, if the police seize evidence from a defendant's home without a search warrant, the lawyer for the defendant can ask the court to exclude the evidence from use at trial. The court holds a hearing to determine whether the search was unreasonable.

If the court rules that key evidence was seized illegally and cannot be used, the government often drops the charges against the defendant.

If the government has a strong case and the court ruled that the evidence was obtained legally, the defendant may decide to plead guilty rather than go to trial, where a conviction is likely.

Deliberations and verdict

After receiving its instructions from the judge, the jury retires to the jury room to discuss the evidence and reach a verdict (a decision on the factual issues). A criminal jury verdict must be unanimous; all jurors must agree that the defendant is guilty or not guilty.

If the jurors cannot agree, the judge declares a mistrial, and the prosecutor must decide whether to ask the court to dismiss the case or have it presented to another jury.

Judgment and sentencing

In federal criminal cases, if the jury (or judge, if there is no jury) decides that the defendant is guilty, the judge sets a date for a sentencing hearing. In federal criminal cases, the jury does not decide whether the defendant will go to prison or for how long; the judge does.

In federal death penalty cases, the jury does decide whether the defendant will receive a death sentence. Sentencing statutes passed by Congress control the judge's sentencing decision. Additionally, judges use Sentencing Guidelines, issued by the U.S. Sentencing Commission, as a source of advice as to the proper sentence. The guidelines consider the nature of the offense and the offender's criminal history.

A presentence report, prepared by one of the court's probation officers, provides the judge with information about the offender and the offense, including the sentence recommended by the guidelines. After determining the sentence, the judge signs a judgment, including the plea, the verdict, and sentence.

Right to appeal

A defendant who is found guilty in a federal criminal trial has a right to appeal the decision to the U.S. court of appeals, that is, ask the court of appeals to review the case to determine whether the trial was conducted properly. The grounds for appeal are usually that the district judge is said to have made an error, either in a procedure (admitting improper evidence, for example) or interpreting the law.

A defendant who pled guilty may not appeal the conviction.

A defendant who pled guilty may have the right to appeal their sentence.

The government may not appeal if a defendant in a criminal case is found not guilty because the Double Jeopardy Clause of the Fifth Amendment to the Constitution provides that no person shall "be twice put in jeopardy of life or limb" for the same offense.

This reflects society's belief that, even if a subsequent trial might finally find a defendant guilty, it is not proper for the government to harass an acquitted defendant through repeated retrials.

However, the government may sometimes appeal a sentence.

Notes for active learning

How Civil and Criminal Appeals Move Through the Federal Courts

Assignment of Judges

Alternative Dispute Resolution (ADR)

Review of Lower Court Decision

Oral Argument

Decision

The Supreme Court of the United States

Assignment of judges

The courts of appeals usually assign cases to a panel of three judges. The panel decides the case for the entire court. Sometimes, when the parties request it or a question of unusual importance, the judges on the appeals court assemble *en banc* (a rare event).

Review of a lower court decision

In making its decision, the panel reviews key parts of the record. The record consists of the documents filed in the case at trial and the transcript of the trial proceedings. The panel learns about the lawyers' legal arguments from the lawyers' briefs.

Briefs are written documents that each side submits to explain its case and tell why the court should decide in its favor.

Oral argument

If the court permits oral argument, the lawyers for each side have a limited amount of time (typically between 15 to 30 minutes) to argue (i.e., advocate and explain) their case to the judges (or justices at the highest court in the jurisdiction) in a formal courtroom session. The judges (or justices for the highest court in the jurisdiction) frequently question the attorneys about the relevant law as it applies to the facts and issues in the case before them.

A court of appeals differs from the federal trial courts. There are no jurors, witnesses, or court reporters. The lawyers for each side, but not the parties, are usually present in the courtroom.

Decision

After the submission of briefs and oral arguments, the judges discuss the case privately, consider relevant *precedents* (court decisions from higher courts in prior cases with similar facts and legal issues), and reach a decision. Courts are required to follow precedents.

For example, a U.S. court of appeals must follow the U.S. Supreme Court's decisions; a district court must follow the decisions of the U.S. Supreme Court and the decisions of the court of appeals of its circuit.

Courts are influenced by decisions they are not required to follow, such as the decisions of other circuits. Courts follow precedent unless they set forth reasons for the diversion.

At least two of the three judges on the panel must agree on a decision. One judge who agrees with the decision is chosen to write an opinion, which announces and explains the decision.

If a judge on the panel disagrees with the majority's opinion, the judge may write a dissent, giving reasons for disagreeing.

Many appellate opinions are published in books of opinions, called reporters. The opinions are read carefully by other judges and lawyers looking for precedents to guide them in their cases.

The accumulated judicial opinions make up a body of law known as *case law*, which is usually an accurate predictor of how future cases will be decided.

For decisions that the judges believe are important to the parties and contribute little to the law, the appeals courts frequently use short, unsigned opinions that often are not published.

If the court of appeals decides that the trial judge incorrectly interpreted the law or followed incorrect procedures, it reverses the district court's decision.

For example, the court of appeals could hold that the district judge allowed the jury to base its decision on evidence that never should have been admitted, and thus the defendant cannot be guilty.

Most of the time, courts of appeals uphold, rather than the reverse, district court decisions.

Sometimes when a higher court reverses the decision of the district court, it sends the case back (i.e., *remand* the case) to the lower court for another trial.

For example, *Miranda v. Arizona* case (1966), the Supreme Court ruled 5-4 that Ernesto Miranda's confession could not be used as evidence because he had not been advised of his right to remain silent or of his right to have a lawyer present during questioning.

However, the government did have other evidence against him. The case was remanded for a new trial, in which the improperly obtained confession was not used as evidence, but the other evidence convicted Miranda.

The Supreme Court of the United States

The Supreme Court is the highest in the nation. It is a different kind of appeals court; its major function is not correcting errors made by trial judges but clarifying the law in cases of national importance or when lower courts disagree about interpreting the Constitution or federal laws.

The Supreme Court does not have to hear every case that it is asked to review. Each year, losing parties ask the Supreme Court to review about 8,000 cases.

Almost all cases come to the Court as a *petition for writ of certiorari*. The court selects only about 80 to 120 of the most significant cases to review with oral arguments.

Supreme Court decisions establish a precedent for interpreting the Constitution and federal laws; holdings that state and federal courts must follow.

The power of judicial review makes the Supreme Court's role in our government vital. Judicial review is the power of a court when deciding a case to declare that a law passed by a legislature or action by the executive branch is invalid because it is inconsistent with the Constitution.

Although district courts, courts of appeals, and state courts can exercise the power of judicial review, their decisions about federal law are always subject, on appeal, to review by the Supreme Court.

When the Supreme Court declares a law unconstitutional, its decision can only be overruled by a later decision of the Supreme Court or Amendment to the Constitution.

Seven of the twenty-seven Amendments to the Constitution have invalidated the decisions of the Supreme Court. However, most Supreme Court cases do not concern the constitutionality of laws, but the interpretation of laws passed by Congress.

Although Congress has steadily increased the number of district and appeals court judges over the years, the Supreme Court has remained the same size since 1869. It consists of a Chief Justice and eight associate justices.

Like the federal court of appeals and federal district judges, the Supreme Court justices are appointed by the President with the Senate's *advice and consent*.

Unlike the judges in the courts of appeals, Supreme Court justices never sit on panels. Absent recusal, nine justices hear cases, and a majority ruling decides cases.

The Supreme Court begins its annual session, or term, on the first Monday of October. The term lasts until the Court has announced its decisions in cases where it has heard an argument that term—usually late June or early July.

During the term, the Court, sitting for two weeks at a time, hears oral arguments on Monday through Wednesday and holds private conferences to discuss the cases, reach decisions, and begin preparing the written opinions that explain its decisions.

Most decisions and opinions are released in the late spring and early summer.

Standards of review for federal courts

Standard of review	De novo	Clearly erroneous	Abuse of discretion
Type of decision under review	Question of the law	Question of fact	Discretionary action
Lower-court decision maker	Trial judge	Trial judge	Trial judge
Deference given to lower court	No deference	Substantial deference	Extreme deference
Party typically benefitted	Appellant	Appellee	Appellee
Definition	An appellate court reviews the legal question anew and independently, without regard to the conclusions reached by the trial court. "When *de novo* review is compelled, no form of appellate deference is acceptable." *Salve Regina College v. Russell,* (1991).	A finding is 'clearly erroneous' when although there is evidence to support it, the reviewing court on the entire evidence is left with the definite and firm conviction that a mistake has been committed. *United States v. United States Gypsum Co.,* (1948) "If the district court's account of the evidence is plausible in light of the record viewed in its entirety, the court of appeals may not reverse it even though convinced that had it been sitting as the trier of fact, it would have weighed the evidence differently. When there are two permissible views of the evidence, the factfinder's choice between them cannot be clearly erroneous." *Anderson v. Bessemer City,* (1985).	Generally, an abuse of discretion only occurs where no reasonable person could take the view adopted by the trial court. If reasonable persons could differ, no abuse of discretion can be found. *Harrington v. DeVito,* (7th Cir. 1981) Under the abuse of discretion standard, a trial court's decision will not be disturbed unless the appellate court has a definite and firm conviction that the lower court made a clear error of judgment or exceeded the bounds of permissible choice in the circumstances. We will not alter a trial court's decision unless it can be shown that the court's decision was an arbitrary, capricious, whimsical, or manifestly unreasonable judgment. *Wright v. Abbott Laboratories, Inc.,* (10th Cir. 2001)
Examples	Motions for summary judgment, constitutional questions, statutory interpretation	Questions regarding who did what, where, and when; questions of intent and motive; questions of ultimate fact (such as negligence)	Rule 11 sanctions, attorney's fees, courtroom management, motions to compel, injunctions, and temporary restraining orders.

The Constitution of the United States (*a transcription*)

THE U.S. NATIONAL ARCHIVES & RECORDS ADMINISTRATION
www.archives.gov

The following text is a transcription of the Constitution as it was inscribed by Jacob Shallus on parchment (the document on display in the Rotunda at the National Archives Museum.) The spelling and punctuation reflect the original.

The Constitution of the United States: A Transcription

The following text is a transcription of the Constitution as it was inscribed by Jacob Shallus on parchment (displayed in the Rotunda at the National Archives Museum.) The authenticated text of the Constitution can be found on the website of the Government Printing Office.

We the People of the United States, in Order to form a more perfect Union, establish Justice, insure domestic Tranquility, provide for the common defence, promote the general Welfare, and secure the Blessings of Liberty to ourselves and our Posterity, do ordain and establish this Constitution for the United States of America.

Article. I

Section. 1.

All legislative Powers herein granted shall be vested in a Congress of the United States, which shall consist of a Senate and House of Representatives.

Section. 2.

The House of Representatives shall be composed of Members chosen every second Year by the People of the several States, and the Electors in each State shall have the Qualifications requisite for Electors of the most numerous Branch of the State Legislature.

No Person shall be a Representative who shall not have attained to the Age of twenty five Years, and been seven Years a Citizen of the United States, and who shall not, when elected, be an Inhabitant of that State in which he shall be chosen.

Representatives and direct Taxes shall be apportioned among the several States which may be included within this Union, according to their respective Numbers, which shall be determined by adding to the whole Number of free Persons, including those bound to Service for a Term of Years, and excluding Indians not taxed, three fifths of all other Persons. The actual Enumeration shall be made within three Years after the first Meeting of the Congress of the United States, and within every subsequent Term of ten Years, in such Manner as they shall by Law direct. The Number of Representatives shall not exceed one for every thirty Thousand, but each State shall have at Least one Representative; and until such enumeration shall be made, the State of New Hampshire shall be entitled to chuse three, Massachusetts eight, Rhode-Island and Providence

Plantations one, Connecticut five, New-York six, New Jersey four, Pennsylvania eight, Delaware one, Maryland six, Virginia ten, North Carolina five, South Carolina five, and Georgia three.

When vacancies happen in the Representation from any State, the Executive Authority thereof shall issue Writs of Election to fill such Vacancies.

The House of Representatives shall chuse their Speaker and other Officers; and shall have the sole Power of Impeachment.

Section. 3.

The Senate of the United States shall be composed of two Senators from each State, chosen by the Legislature thereof, for six Years; and each Senator shall have one Vote.

Immediately after they shall be assembled in Consequence of the first Election, they shall be divided as equally as may be into three Classes. The Seats of the Senators of the first Class shall be vacated at the Expiration of the second Year, of the second Class at the Expiration of the fourth Year, and of the third Class at the Expiration of the sixth Year, so that one third may be chosen every second Year; and if Vacancies happen by Resignation, or otherwise, during the Recess of the Legislature of any State, the Executive thereof may make temporary Appointments until the next Meeting of the Legislature, which shall then fill such Vacancies.

No Person shall be a Senator who shall not have attained to the Age of thirty Years, and been nine Years a Citizen of the United States, and who shall not, when elected, be an Inhabitant of that State for which he shall be chosen.

The Vice President of the United States shall be President of the Senate, but shall have no Vote, unless they be equally divided.

The Senate shall chuse their other Officers, and also a President pro tempore, in the Absence of the Vice President, or when he shall exercise the Office of President of the United States.

The Senate shall have the sole Power to try all Impeachments. When sitting for that Purpose, they shall be on Oath or Affirmation. When the President of the United States is tried, the Chief Justice shall preside: And no Person shall be convicted without the Concurrence of two thirds of the Members present.

Judgment in Cases of Impeachment shall not extend further than to removal from Office, and disqualification to hold and enjoy any Office of honor, Trust or Profit under the United States: but the Party convicted shall nevertheless be liable and subject to Indictment, Trial, Judgment and Punishment, according to Law.

Section. 4.

The Times, Places and Manner of holding Elections for Senators and Representatives, shall be prescribed in each State by the Legislature thereof; but the Congress may at any time by Law make or alter such Regulations, except as to the Places of chusing Senators.

The Congress shall assemble at least once in every Year, and such Meeting shall be on the first Monday in December, unless they shall by Law appoint a different Day.

Section. 5.

Each House shall be the Judge of the Elections, Returns and Qualifications of its own Members, and a Majority of each shall constitute a Quorum to do Business; but a smaller Number may adjourn from day to day, and may be authorized to compel the Attendance of absent Members, in such Manner, and under such Penalties as each House may provide.

Each House may determine the Rules of its Proceedings, punish its Members for disorderly Behaviour, and, with the Concurrence of two thirds, expel a Member.

Each House shall keep a Journal of its Proceedings, and from time to time publish the same, excepting such Parts as may in their Judgment require Secrecy; and the Yeas and Nays of the Members of either House on any question shall, at the Desire of one fifth of those Present, be entered on the Journal.

Neither House, during the Session of Congress, shall, without the Consent of the other, adjourn for more than three days, nor to any other Place than that in which the two Houses shall be sitting.

Section. 6.

The Senators and Representatives shall receive a Compensation for their Services, to be ascertained by Law, and paid out of the Treasury of the United States. They shall in all Cases, except Treason, Felony and Breach of the Peace, be privileged from Arrest during their Attendance at the Session of their respective Houses, and in going to and returning from the same; and for any Speech or Debate in either House, they shall not be questioned in any other Place.

No Senator or Representative shall, during the Time for which he was elected, be appointed to any civil Office under the Authority of the United States, which shall have been created, or the Emoluments whereof shall have been encreased during such time; and no Person holding any Office under the United States, shall be a Member of either House during his Continuance in Office.

Section. 7.

All Bills for raising Revenue shall originate in the House of Representatives; but the Senate may propose or concur with Amendments as on other Bills.

Every Bill which shall have passed the House of Representatives and the Senate, shall, before it become a Law, be presented to the President of the United States; If he approves he shall sign it, but if not he shall return it, with his Objections to that House in which it shall have originated, who shall enter the Objections at large on their Journal, and proceed to reconsider it. If after such Reconsideration two thirds of that House shall agree to pass the Bill, it shall be sent, together with the Objections, to the other House, by which it shall likewise be reconsidered, and if approved by two thirds of that House, it shall become a Law. But in all such Cases the Votes of both Houses shall be determined by yeas and Nays, and the Names of the Persons voting for and against the Bill shall be entered on the Journal of each House respectively. If any Bill shall not be returned by the President within ten Days (Sundays excepted) after it shall have been presented to him, the Same shall be a Law, in like Manner as if he had signed it, unless the Congress by their Adjournment prevent its Return, in which Case it shall not be a Law.

Every Order, Resolution, or Vote to which the Concurrence of the Senate and House of Representatives may be necessary (except on a question of Adjournment) shall be presented to the President of the United States; and before the Same shall take Effect, shall be approved by him, or being disapproved by him, shall be repassed by two thirds of the Senate and House of Representatives, according to the Rules and Limitations prescribed in the Case of a Bill.

Section. 8.

The Congress shall have Power To lay and collect Taxes, Duties, Imposts and Excises, to pay the Debts and provide for the common Defence and general Welfare of the United States; but all Duties, Imposts and Excises shall be uniform throughout the United States;

To borrow Money on the credit of the United States;

To regulate Commerce with foreign Nations, and among the several States, and with the Indian Tribes;

To establish an uniform Rule of Naturalization, and uniform Laws on the subject of Bankruptcies throughout the United States;

To coin Money, regulate the Value thereof, and of foreign Coin, and fix the Standard of Weights and Measures;

To provide for the Punishment of counterfeiting the Securities and current Coin of the United States;

To establish Post Offices and post Roads;

To promote the Progress of Science and useful Arts, by securing for limited Times to Authors and Inventors the exclusive Right to their respective Writings and Discoveries;

To constitute Tribunals inferior to the Supreme Court;

To define and punish Piracies and Felonies committed on the high Seas, and Offences against the Law of Nations;

To declare War, grant Letters of Marque and Reprisal, and make Rules concerning Captures on Land and Water;

To raise and support Armies, but no Appropriation of Money to that Use shall be for a longer Term than two Years;

To provide and maintain a Navy;

To make Rules for the Government and Regulation of the land and naval Forces;

To provide for calling forth the Militia to execute the Laws of the Union, suppress Insurrections and repel Invasions;

To provide for organizing, arming, and disciplining, the Militia, and for governing such Part of them as may be employed in the Service of the United States, reserving to the States respectively, the Appointment of the Officers, and the Authority of training the Militia according to the discipline prescribed by Congress;

To exercise exclusive Legislation in all Cases whatsoever, over such District (not exceeding ten Miles square) as may, by Cession of particular States, and the Acceptance of Congress, become the Seat of the Government of the United States, and to exercise like Authority over all Places purchased by the Consent of the Legislature of the State in which the Same shall be, for the Erection of Forts, Magazines, Arsenals, dock-Yards, and other needful Buildings;—And

To make all Laws which shall be necessary and proper for carrying into Execution the foregoing Powers, and all other Powers vested by this Constitution in the Government of the United States, or in any Department or Officer thereof.

Section. 9.

The Migration or Importation of such Persons as any of the States now existing shall think proper to admit, shall not be prohibited by the Congress prior to the Year one thousand eight hundred and eight, but a Tax or duty may be imposed on such Importation, not exceeding ten dollars for each Person.

The Privilege of the Writ of Habeas Corpus shall not be suspended, unless when in Cases of Rebellion or Invasion the public Safety may require it.

No Bill of Attainder or ex post facto Law shall be passed.

No Capitation, or other direct, Tax shall be laid, unless in Proportion to the Census or enumeration herein before directed to be taken.

No Tax or Duty shall be laid on Articles exported from any State.

No Preference shall be given by any Regulation of Commerce or Revenue to the Ports of one State over those of another: nor shall Vessels bound to, or from, one State, be obliged to enter, clear, or pay Duties in another.

No Money shall be drawn from the Treasury, but in Consequence of Appropriations made by Law; and a regular Statement and Account of the Receipts and Expenditures of all public Money shall be published from time to time.

No Title of Nobility shall be granted by the United States: And no Person holding any Office of Profit or Trust under them, shall, without the Consent of the Congress, accept of any present, Emolument, Office, or Title, of any kind whatever, from any King, Prince, or foreign State.

Section. 10.

No State shall enter into any Treaty, Alliance, or Confederation; grant Letters of Marque and Reprisal; coin Money; emit Bills of Credit; make any Thing but gold and silver Coin a Tender in Payment of Debts; pass any Bill of Attainder, ex post facto Law, or Law impairing the Obligation of Contracts, or grant any Title of Nobility.

No State shall, without the Consent of the Congress, lay any Imposts or Duties on Imports or Exports, except what may be absolutely necessary for executing it's inspection Laws: and the net

Produce of all Duties and Imposts, laid by any State on Imports or Exports, shall be for the Use of the Treasury of the United States; and all such Laws shall be subject to the Revision and Controul of the Congress.

No State shall, without the Consent of Congress, lay any Duty of Tonnage, keep Troops, or Ships of War in time of Peace, enter into any Agreement or Compact with another State, or with a foreign Power, or engage in War, unless actually invaded, or in such imminent Danger as will not admit of delay.

Article. II

Section. 1.

The executive Power shall be vested in a President of the United States of America. He shall hold his Office during the Term of four Years, and, together with the Vice President, chosen for the same Term, be elected, as follows

Each State shall appoint, in such Manner as the Legislature thereof may direct, a Number of Electors, equal to the whole Number of Senators and Representatives to which the State may be entitled in the Congress: but no Senator or Representative, or Person holding an Office of Trust or Profit under the United States, shall be appointed an Elector.

The Electors shall meet in their respective States, and vote by Ballot for two Persons, of whom one at least shall not be an Inhabitant of the same State with themselves. And they shall make a List of all the Persons voted for, and of the Number of Votes for each; which List they shall sign and certify, and transmit sealed to the Seat of the Government of the United States, directed to the President of the Senate. The President of the Senate shall, in the Presence of the Senate and House of Representatives, open all the Certificates, and the Votes shall then be counted. The Person having the greatest Number of Votes shall be the President, if such Number be a Majority of the whole Number of Electors appointed; and if there be more than one who have such Majority, and have an equal Number of Votes, then the House of Representatives shall immediately chuse by Ballot one of them for President; and if no Person have a Majority, then from the five highest on the List the said House shall in like Manner chuse the President. But in chusing the President, the Votes shall be taken by States, the Representation from each State having one Vote; A quorum for this Purpose shall consist of a Member or Members from two thirds of the States, and a Majority of all the States shall be necessary to a Choice. In every Case, after the Choice of the President, the Person having the greatest Number of Votes of the Electors shall be the Vice President. But if there should remain two or more who have equal Votes, the Senate shall chuse from them by Ballot the Vice President.

The Congress may determine the Time of chusing the Electors, and the Day on which they shall give their Votes; which Day shall be the same throughout the United States.

No Person except a natural born Citizen, or a Citizen of the United States, at the time of the Adoption of this Constitution, shall be eligible to the Office of President; neither shall any Person be eligible to that Office who shall not have attained to the Age of thirty five Years, and been fourteen Years a Resident within the United States.

In Case of the Removal of the President from Office, or of his Death, Resignation, or Inability to discharge the Powers and Duties of the said Office, the Same shall devolve on the Vice President, and the Congress may by Law provide for the Case of Removal, Death, Resignation or Inability, both of the President and Vice President, declaring what Officer shall then act as President, and such Officer shall act accordingly, until the Disability be removed, or a President shall be elected.

The President shall, at stated Times, receive for his Services, a Compensation, which shall neither be encreased nor diminished during the Period for which he shall have been elected, and he shall not receive within that Period any other Emolument from the United States, or any of them.

Before he enters on the Execution of his Office, he shall take the following Oath or Affirmation:—"I do solemnly swear (or affirm) that I will faithfully execute the Office of President of the United States, and will to the best of my Ability, preserve, protect and defend the Constitution of the United States."

Section. 2.

The President shall be Commander in Chief of the Army and Navy of the United States, and of the Militia of the several States, when called into the actual Service of the United States; he may require the Opinion, in writing, of the principal Officer in each of the executive Departments, upon any Subject relating to the Duties of their respective Offices, and he shall have Power to grant Reprieves and Pardons for Offences against the United States, except in Cases of Impeachment.

He shall have Power, by and with the Advice and Consent of the Senate, to make Treaties, provided two thirds of the Senators present concur; and he shall nominate, and by and with the Advice and Consent of the Senate, shall appoint Ambassadors, other public Ministers and Consuls, Judges of the supreme Court, and all other Officers of the United States, whose Appointments are not herein otherwise provided for, and which shall be established by Law: but the Congress may by Law vest the Appointment of such inferior Officers, as they think proper, in the President alone, in the Courts of Law, or in the Heads of Departments.

The President shall have Power to fill up all Vacancies that may happen during the Recess of the Senate, by granting Commissions which shall expire at the End of their next Session.

Section. 3.

He shall from time to time give to the Congress Information of the State of the Union, and recommend to their Consideration such Measures as he shall judge necessary and expedient; he may, on extraordinary Occasions, convene both Houses, or either of them, and in Case of Disagreement between them, with Respect to the Time of Adjournment, he may adjourn them to such Time as he shall think proper; he shall receive Ambassadors and other public Ministers; he shall take Care that the Laws be faithfully executed, and shall Commission all the Officers of the United States.

Section. 4.

The President, Vice President and all civil Officers of the United States, shall be removed from Office on Impeachment for, and Conviction of, Treason, Bribery, or other high Crimes and Misdemeanors.

Article III

Section. 1.

The judicial Power of the United States, shall be vested in one supreme Court, and in such inferior Courts as the Congress may from time to time ordain and establish. The Judges, both of the supreme and inferior Courts, shall hold their Offices during good Behaviour, and shall, at stated Times, receive for their Services, a Compensation, which shall not be diminished during their Continuance in Office.

Section. 2.

The judicial Power shall extend to all Cases, in Law and Equity, arising under this Constitution, the Laws of the United States, and Treaties made, or which shall be made, under their Authority;—to all Cases affecting Ambassadors, other public Ministers and Consuls;—to all Cases of admiralty and maritime Jurisdiction;—to Controversies to which the United States shall be a Party;—to Controversies between two or more States;—between a State and Citizens of another State,—between Citizens of different States,—between Citizens of the same State claiming Lands under Grants of different States, and between a State, or the Citizens thereof, and foreign States, Citizens or Subjects.

In all Cases affecting Ambassadors, other public Ministers and Consuls, and those in which a State shall be Party, the supreme Court shall have original Jurisdiction. In all the other Cases before mentioned, the supreme Court shall have appellate Jurisdiction, both as to Law and Fact, with such Exceptions, and under such Regulations as the Congress shall make.

The Trial of all Crimes, except in Cases of Impeachment, shall be by Jury; and such Trial shall be held in the State where the said Crimes shall have been committed; but when not committed within any State, the Trial shall be at such Place or Places as the Congress may by Law have directed.

Section. 3.

Treason against the United States, shall consist only in levying War against them, or in adhering to their Enemies, giving them Aid and Comfort. No Person shall be convicted of Treason unless on the Testimony of two Witnesses to the same overt Act, or on Confession in open Court.

The Congress shall have Power to declare the Punishment of Treason, but no Attainder of Treason shall work Corruption of Blood, or Forfeiture except during the Life of the Person attainted.

Article. IV

Section. 1.

Full Faith and Credit shall be given in each State to the public Acts, Records, and judicial Proceedings of every other State. And the Congress may by general Laws prescribe the Manner in which such Acts, Records and Proceedings shall be proved, and the Effect thereof.

Section. 2.

The Citizens of each State shall be entitled to all Privileges and Immunities of Citizens in the several States.

A Person charged in any State with Treason, Felony, or other Crime, who shall flee from Justice, and be found in another State, shall on Demand of the executive Authority of the State from which he fled, be delivered up, to be removed to the State having Jurisdiction of the Crime.

No Person held to Service or Labour in one State, under the Laws thereof, escaping into another, shall, in Consequence of any Law or Regulation therein, be discharged from such Service or Labour, but shall be delivered up on Claim of the Party to whom such Service or Labour may be due.

Section. 3.

New States may be admitted by the Congress into this Union; but no new State shall be formed or erected within the Jurisdiction of any other State; nor any State be formed by the Junction of two or more States, or Parts of States, without the Consent of the Legislatures of the States concerned as well as of the Congress.

The Congress shall have Power to dispose of and make all needful Rules and Regulations respecting the Territory or other Property belonging to the United States; and nothing in this Constitution shall be so construed as to Prejudice any Claims of the United States, or of any particular State.

Section. 4.

The United States shall guarantee to every State in this Union a Republican Form of Government, and shall protect each of them against Invasion; and on Application of the Legislature, or of the Executive (when the Legislature cannot be convened), against domestic Violence.

Article. V

The Congress, whenever two thirds of both Houses shall deem it necessary, shall propose Amendments to this Constitution, or, on the Application of the Legislatures of two thirds of the several States, shall call a Convention for proposing Amendments, which, in either Case, shall be valid to all Intents and Purposes, as Part of this Constitution, when ratified by the Legislatures of three fourths of the several States, or by Conventions in three fourths thereof, as the one or the other Mode of Ratification may be proposed by the Congress; Provided that no Amendment which may be made prior to the Year One thousand eight hundred and eight shall in any Manner affect the first and fourth Clauses in the Ninth Section of the first Article; and that no State, without its Consent, shall be deprived of its equal Suffrage in the Senate.

Article. VI

All Debts contracted and Engagements entered into, before the Adoption of this Constitution, shall be as valid against the United States under this Constitution, as under the Confederation.

This Constitution, and the Laws of the United States which shall be made in Pursuance thereof; and all Treaties made, or which shall be made, under the Authority of the United States, shall be the supreme Law of the Land; and the Judges in every State shall be bound thereby, any Thing in the Constitution or Laws of any State to the Contrary notwithstanding.

The Senators and Representatives before mentioned, and the Members of the several State Legislatures, and all executive and judicial Officers, both of the United States and of the several States, shall be bound by Oath or Affirmation, to support this Constitution; but no religious Test shall ever be required as a Qualification to any Office or public Trust under the United States.

Article. VII

The Ratification of the Conventions of nine States, shall be sufficient for the Establishment of this Constitution between the States so ratifying the Same.

The Word, "the," being interlined between the seventh and eighth Lines of the first Page, The Word "Thirty" being partly written on an Erazure in the fifteenth Line of the first Page, The Words "is tried" being interlined between the thirty second and thirty third Lines of the first Page and the Word "the" being interlined between the forty third and forty fourth Lines of the second Page.

Attest William Jackson Secretary, done in Convention by the Unanimous Consent of the States present the Seventeenth Day of September in the Year of our Lord one thousand seven hundred and Eighty seven and of the Independance of the United States of America the Twelfth In witness whereof We have hereunto subscribed our Names, G°. Washington, *Presidt and deputy from Virginia*

Delaware
Geo: Read
Gunning Bedford jun
John Dickinson
Richard Bassett
Jaco: Broom

Maryland
James McHenry
Dan of St Thos.
Jenifer
Danl. Carroll

Virginia
John Blair
James Madison Jr.

North Carolina
Wm. Blount
Richd. Dobbs
Spaight
Hu Williamson

South Carolina
J. Rutledge
Charles Cotesworth
Pinckney
Charles Pinckney
Pierce Butler

Georgia
William Few
Abr Baldwin

New Hampshire
John Langdon
Nicholas Gilman

Massachusetts
Nathaniel Gorham
Rufus King

Connecticut
Wm. Saml. Johnson
Roger Sherman

New York
Alexander Hamilton

New Jersey
Wil: Livingston
David Brearley
Wm. Paterson
Jona: Dayton

Pensylvania
B Franklin
Thomas Mifflin
Robt. Morris
Geo. Clymer
Thos. FitzSimons
Jared Ingersoll
James Wilson
Gouv Morris

Enactment of the Bill of Rights of the United States of America (1791)

The first ten Amendments to the Constitution make up the Bill of Rights. Written by James Madison in response to calls from several states for greater constitutional protection for individual liberties, the Bill of Rights lists specific prohibitions on governmental power. The Virginia Declaration of Rights, written by George Mason, strongly influenced Madison.

One of the contention points between Federalists and Anti-Federalists was the Constitution's lack of a bill of rights that would place specific limits on government power.

Federalists argued that the Constitution did not need a bill of rights because the people and the states kept powers not explicitly given to the federal government.

Anti-Federalists held that a *bill of rights* was necessary to safeguard individual liberty.

Madison, then a member of the U.S. House of Representatives, went through the Constitution itself, making changes where he thought most appropriate.

Several Representatives, led by Roger Sherman, objected that Congress had no authority to change the wording of the Constitution. Therefore, Madison's changes were presented as a list of amendments that would follow Article VII.

The House approved 17 amendments. Of these 17, the Senate approved 12. Those 12 were sent to the states for approval in August of 1789. Of those 12 proposed amendments, 10 were quickly ratified. Virginia's legislature became the last to ratify the Amendments on December 15, 1791. These Amendments are the Bill of Rights.

The Bill of Rights is a list of limits on government power. For example, what the Founders saw as the natural right of individuals to speak and worship freely was protected by the First Amendment's prohibitions on Congress from making laws establishing a religion or abridging freedom of speech.

Another example is the natural right to be free from the government's unreasonable intrusion in one's home was safeguarded by the Fourth Amendment's warrant requirements.

Other precursors to the Bill of Rights include English documents such as the Magna Carta[1], the Petition of Rights, the English Bill of Rights, and the Massachusetts Body of Liberties.

The Magna Carta illustrates Compact Theory[1] as well as initial strides toward limited government. Its provisions address individual rights and political rights. Latin for "Great Charter," the Magna Carta was written by Barons in Runnymede, England, and forced on the King.

Although the protections were generally limited to the prerogatives of the Barons, the Magna Carta embodied the general principle that the King accepted limitations on his rule. These included the fundamental acknowledgment that the king was not above the law.

Included in the Magna Carta are protections for the English church, petitioning the king, freedom from the forced quarter of troops and unreasonable searches, due process and fair trial protections, and freedom from excessive fines. These protections can be found in the First, Third, Fourth, Fifth, Sixth, and Eighth Amendments to the Constitution.

The Magna Carta is the oldest compact in England. The Mayflower Compact, the Fundamental Orders of Connecticut, and the Albany Plan are examples from the American colonies.

The Articles of Confederation was a compact among the states, and the Constitution creates a compact based on a federal system between the national government, state governments, and the people. The Hayne-Webster Debate focused on the compact created by the Constitution.

---

[1] Philosophers including Thomas Hobbes, John Locke, and Jean-Jacques Rousseau theorized that peoples' condition in a "state of nature" (that is, outside of society) is one of freedom, but that freedom inevitably degrades into war, chaos, or debilitating competition without the benefit of a system of laws and government. They reasoned, therefore, that for their happiness, individuals willingly trade some of their natural freedom in exchange for the protections provided by the government.

The Bill of Rights: Amendments I–X

Amendment I

Congress shall make no law respecting an establishment of religion, or prohibiting the free exercise thereof; or abridging the freedom of speech, or of the press; or the right of the people peaceably to assemble, and to petition the government for a redress of grievances.

Amendment II

A well regulated militia, being necessary to the security of a free state, the right of the people to keep and bear arms, shall not be infringed.

Amendment III

No soldier shall, in time of peace be quartered in any house, without the consent of the owner, nor in time of war, but in a manner to be prescribed by law.

Amendment IV

The right of the people to be secure in their persons, houses, papers, and effects, against unreasonable searches and seizures, shall not be violated, and no warrants shall issue, but upon probable cause, supported by oath or affirmation, and particularly describing the place to be searched, and the persons or things to be seized.

Amendment V

No person shall be held to answer for a capital, or otherwise infamous crime, unless on a presentment or indictment of a grand jury, except in cases arising in the land or naval forces, or in the militia, when in actual service in time of war or public danger; nor shall any person be subject for the same offense to be twice put in jeopardy of life or limb; nor shall be compelled in any criminal case to be a witness against himself, nor be deprived of life, liberty, or property, without due process of law; nor shall private property be taken for public use, without just compensation.

Amendment VI

In all criminal prosecutions, the accused shall enjoy the right to a speedy and public trial, by an impartial jury of the state and district wherein the crime shall have been committed, which district shall have been previously ascertained by law, and to be informed of the nature and cause of the accusation; to be confronted with the witnesses against him; to have compulsory process for obtaining witnesses in his favor, and to have the assistance of counsel for his defense.

Amendment VII

In suits at common law, where the value in controversy shall exceed twenty dollars, the right of trial by jury shall be preserved, and no fact tried by a jury, shall be otherwise reexamined in any court of the United States, than according to the rules of the common law.

Amendment VIII

Excessive bail shall not be required, nor excessive fines imposed, nor cruel and unusual punishments inflicted.

Amendment IX

The enumeration in the Constitution, of certain rights, shall not be construed to deny or disparage others retained by the people.

Amendment X

The powers not delegated to the United States by the Constitution, nor prohibited by it to the states, are reserved to the states respectively, or to the people.

Constitutional Amendments XI–XXVII

AMENDMENT XI

Passed by Congress March 4, 1794. Ratified February 7, 1795.

Note: Article III, section 2, of the Constitution was modified by amendment 11.

The Judicial power of the United States shall not be construed to extend to any suit in law or equity, commenced or prosecuted against one of the United States by Citizens of another State, or by Citizens or Subjects of any Foreign State.

AMENDMENT XII

Passed by Congress December 9, 1803. Ratified June 15, 1804.

Note: A portion of Article II, section 1 of the Constitution was superseded by the 12th amendment.

The Electors shall meet in their respective states and vote by ballot for President and Vice-President, one of whom, at least, shall not be an inhabitant of the same state with themselves; they shall name in their ballots the person voted for as President, and in distinct ballots the person voted for as Vice-President, and they shall make distinct lists of all persons voted for as President, and of all persons voted for as Vice-President, and of the number of votes for each, which lists they shall sign and certify, and transmit sealed to the seat of the government of the United States, directed to the President of the Senate; -- the President of the Senate shall, in the presence of the Senate and House of Representatives, open all the certificates and the votes shall then be counted; -- The person having the greatest number of votes for President, shall be the President, if such number be a majority of the whole number of Electors appointed; and if no person have such majority, then from the persons having the highest numbers not exceeding three on the list of those voted for as President, the House of Representatives shall choose immediately, by ballot, the President. But in choosing the President, the votes shall be taken by states, the representation from each state having one vote; a quorum for this purpose shall consist of a member or members from two-thirds of the states, and a majority of all the states shall be necessary to a choice. [And if the House of Representatives shall not choose a President whenever the right of choice shall devolve upon them, before the fourth day of March next following, then the Vice-President shall act as President, as in case of the death or other constitutional disability of the President. --]* The person having the greatest number of votes as Vice-President, shall be the Vice-President, if such number be a majority of the whole number of Electors appointed, and if no person have a majority, then from the two highest numbers on the list, the Senate shall choose the Vice-President; a quorum for the purpose shall consist of two-thirds of the whole number of Senators, and a majority of the whole number shall be necessary to a choice. But no person constitutionally ineligible to the office of President shall be eligible to that of Vice-President of the United States.

*Superseded by section 3 of the 20th Amendment.

AMENDMENT XIII

Passed by Congress January 31, 1865. Ratified December 6, 1865.

Note: A portion of Article IV, section 2, of the Constitution was superseded by the 13th amendment.

Section 1.
Neither slavery nor involuntary servitude, except as a punishment for crime whereof the party shall have been duly convicted, shall exist within the United States, or any place subject to their jurisdiction.

Section 2.
Congress shall have power to enforce this article by appropriate legislation.

AMENDMENT XIV

Passed by Congress June 13, 1866. Ratified July 9, 1868.

Note: Article I, section 2, of the Constitution was modified by section 2 of the 14th amendment.

Section 1.
All persons born or naturalized in the United States, and subject to the jurisdiction thereof, are citizens of the United States and of the State wherein they reside. No State shall make or enforce any law which shall abridge the privileges or immunities of citizens of the United States; nor shall any State deprive any person of life, liberty, or property, without due process of law; nor deny to any person within its jurisdiction the equal protection of the laws.

Section 2.
Representatives shall be apportioned among the several States according to their respective numbers, counting the whole number of persons in each State, excluding Indians not taxed. But when the right to vote at any election for the choice of electors for President and Vice-President of the United States, Representatives in Congress, the Executive and Judicial officers of a State, or the members of the Legislature thereof, is denied to any of the male inhabitants of such State, being twenty-one years of age,* and citizens of the United States, or in any way abridged, except for participation in rebellion, or other crime, the basis of representation therein shall be reduced in the proportion which the number of such male citizens shall bear to the whole number of male citizens twenty-one years of age in such State.

Section 3.
No person shall be a Senator or Representative in Congress, or elector of President and Vice-President, or hold any office, civil or military, under the United States, or under any State, who, having previously taken an oath, as a member of Congress, or as an officer of the United States, or as a member of any State legislature, or as an executive or judicial officer of any State, to support the Constitution of the United States, shall have engaged in insurrection or rebellion against the same, or given aid or comfort to the enemies thereof. But Congress may by a vote of two-thirds of each House, remove such disability.

Section 4.

The validity of the public debt of the United States, authorized by law, including debts incurred for payment of pensions and bounties for services in suppressing insurrection or rebellion, shall not be questioned. But neither the United States nor any State shall assume or pay any debt or obligation incurred in aid of insurrection or rebellion against the United States, or any claim for the loss or emancipation of any slave; but all such debts, obligations and claims shall be held illegal and void.

Section 5.

The Congress shall have the power to enforce, by appropriate legislation, the provisions of this article.

*Changed by section 1 of the 26th Amendment.

AMENDMENT XV

Passed by Congress February 26, 1869. Ratified February 3, 1870.

Section 1.

The right of citizens of the United States to vote shall not be denied or abridged by the United States or by any State on account of race, color, or previous condition of servitude.

Section 2.

The Congress shall have the power to enforce this article by appropriate legislation.

AMENDMENT XVI

Passed by Congress July 2, 1909. Ratified February 3, 1913.

Note: Article I, section 9, of the Constitution was modified by amendment 16.

The Congress shall have power to lay and collect taxes on incomes, from whatever source derived, without apportionment among the several States, and without regard to any census or enumeration.

AMENDMENT XVII

Passed by Congress May 13, 1912. Ratified April 8, 1913.

Note: Article I, section 3, of the Constitution was modified by the 17th Amendment.

The Senate of the United States shall be composed of two Senators from each State, elected by the people thereof, for six years; and each Senator shall have one vote. The electors in each State shall have the qualifications requisite for electors of the most numerous branch of the State legislatures.

When vacancies happen in the representation of any State in the Senate, the executive authority of such State shall issue writs of election to fill such vacancies: *Provided*, That the legislature of any State may empower the executive thereof to make temporary appointments until the people fill the vacancies by election as the legislature may direct.

This amendment shall not be so construed as to affect the election or term of any Senator chosen before it becomes valid as part of the Constitution.

AMENDMENT XVIII

Passed by Congress December 18, 1917. Ratified January 16, 1919. Repealed by Amendment 21.

Section 1.

After one year from the ratification of this article the manufacture, sale, or transportation of intoxicating liquors within, the importation thereof into, or the exportation thereof from the United States and all territory subject to the jurisdiction thereof for beverage purposes is hereby prohibited.

Section 2.

The Congress and the several States shall have concurrent power to enforce this article by appropriate legislation.

Section 3.

This article shall be inoperative unless it shall have been ratified as an amendment to the Constitution by the legislatures of the several States, as provided in the Constitution, within seven years from the date of the submission hereof to the States by the Congress.

AMENDMENT XIX

Passed by Congress June 4, 1919. Ratified August 18, 1920.

The right of citizens of the United States to vote shall not be denied or abridged by the United States or by any State on account of sex.

Congress shall have power to enforce this article by appropriate legislation.

AMENDMENT XX

Passed by Congress March 2, 1932. Ratified January 23, 1933.

Note: Article I, section 4, of the Constitution was modified by section 2 of this Amendment. In addition, a portion of the 12th Amendment was superseded by section 3.

Section 1.

The terms of the President and the Vice President shall end at noon on the 20th day of January, and the terms of Senators and Representatives at noon on the 3d day of January, of the years in which such terms would have ended if this article had not been ratified; and the terms of their successors shall then begin.

Section 2.

The Congress shall assemble at least once in every year, and such meeting shall begin at noon on the 3d day of January, unless they shall by law appoint a different day.

Section 3.

If, at the time fixed for the beginning of the term of the President, the President elect shall have died, the Vice President elect shall become President. If a President shall not have been chosen before the time fixed for the beginning of his term, or if the President elect shall have failed to qualify, then the Vice President elect shall act as President until a President shall have qualified; and the Congress may by law provide for the case wherein neither a President elect nor a Vice President elect shall have qualified, declaring who shall then act as President, or the manner in which one who is to act shall be selected, and such person shall act accordingly until a President or Vice President shall have qualified.

Section 4.

The Congress may by law provide for the case of the death of any of the persons from whom the House of Representatives may choose a President whenever the right of choice shall have devolved upon them, and for the case of the death of any of the persons from whom the Senate may choose a Vice President whenever the right of choice shall have devolved upon them.

Section 5.

Sections 1 and 2 shall take effect on the 15th day of October following the ratification of this article.

Section 6.

This article shall be inoperative unless it shall have been ratified as an amendment to the Constitution by the legislatures of three-fourths of the several States within seven years from the date of its submission.

AMENDMENT XXI

Passed by Congress February 20, 1933. Ratified December 5, 1933.

Section 1.

The eighteenth article of amendment to the Constitution of the United States is hereby repealed.

Section 2.

The transportation or importation into any State, Territory, or possession of the United States for delivery or use therein of intoxicating liquors, in violation of the laws thereof, is hereby prohibited.

Section 3.

This article shall be inoperative unless it shall have been ratified as an amendment to the Constitution by conventions in the several States, as provided in the Constitution, within seven years from the date of the submission hereof to the States by the Congress.

AMENDMENT XXII

Passed by Congress March 21, 1947. Ratified February 27, 1951.

Section 1.

No person shall be elected to the office of the President more than twice, and no person who has held the office of President, or acted as President, for more than two years of a term to which some other person was elected President shall be elected to the office of the President more than once. But this Article shall not apply to any person holding the office of President when this Article was proposed by the Congress, and shall not prevent any person who may be holding the office of President, or acting as President, during the term within which this Article becomes operative from holding the office of President or acting as President during the remainder of such term.

Section 2.

This article shall be inoperative unless it shall have been ratified as an amendment to the Constitution by the legislatures of three-fourths of the several States within seven years from the date of its submission to the States by the Congress.

AMENDMENT XXIII

Passed by Congress June 16, 1960. Ratified March 29, 1961.

Section 1.

The District constituting the seat of Government of the United States shall appoint in such manner as the Congress may direct:

A number of electors of President and Vice President equal to the whole number of Senators and Representatives in Congress to which the District would be entitled if it were a State, but in no event more than the least populous State; they shall be in addition to those appointed by the States, but they shall be considered, for the purposes of the election of President and Vice President, to be electors appointed by a State; and they shall meet in the District and perform such duties as provided by the twelfth article of amendment.

Section 2.

The Congress shall have power to enforce this article by appropriate legislation.

AMENDMENT XXIV

Passed by Congress August 27, 1962. Ratified January 23, 1964.

Section 1.

The right of citizens of the United States to vote in any primary or other election for President or Vice President, for electors for President or Vice President, or for Senator or Representative in Congress, shall not be denied or abridged by the United States or any State by reason of failure to pay any poll tax or other tax.

Section 2.

The Congress shall have power to enforce this article by appropriate legislation.

AMENDMENT XXV

Passed by Congress July 6, 1965. Ratified February 10, 1967.

Note: Article II, section 1, of the Constitution was affected by the 25th amendment.

Section 1.

In case of the removal of the President from office or of his death or resignation, the Vice President shall become President.

Section 2.

Whenever there is a vacancy in the office of the Vice President, the President shall nominate a Vice President who shall take office upon confirmation by a majority vote of both Houses of Congress.

Section 3.

Whenever the President transmits to the President pro tempore of the Senate and the Speaker of the House of Representatives his written declaration that he is unable to discharge the powers and duties of his office, and until he transmits to them a written declaration to the contrary, such powers and duties shall be discharged by the Vice President as Acting President.

Section 4.

Whenever the Vice President and a majority of either the principal officers of the executive departments or of such other body as Congress may by law provide, transmit to the President pro tempore of the Senate and the Speaker of the House of Representatives their written declaration that the President is unable to discharge the powers and duties of his office, the Vice President shall immediately assume the powers and duties of the office as Acting President.

Thereafter, when the President transmits to the President pro tempore of the Senate and the Speaker of the House of Representatives his written declaration that no inability exists, he shall resume the powers and duties of his office unless the Vice President and a majority of either the principal officers of the executive department or of such other body as Congress may by law provide, transmit within four days to the President pro tempore of the Senate and the Speaker of the House of Representatives their written declaration that the President is unable to discharge the powers and duties of his office. Thereupon Congress shall decide the issue, assembling within forty-eight hours for that purpose if not in session. If the Congress, within twenty-one days after receipt of the latter written declaration, or, if Congress is not in session, within twenty-one days after Congress is required to assemble, determines by two-thirds vote of both Houses that the President is unable to discharge the powers and duties of his office, the Vice President shall continue to discharge the same as Acting President; otherwise, the President shall resume the powers and duties of his office.

AMENDMENT XXVI

Passed by Congress March 23, 1971. Ratified July 1, 1971.

Note: Amendment 14, section 2, of the Constitution was modified by section 1 of the 26th amendment.

Section 1.
The right of citizens of the United States, who are eighteen years of age or older, to vote shall not be denied or abridged by the United States or by any State on account of age.

Section 2.
The Congress shall have power to enforce this article by appropriate legislation.

AMENDMENT XXVII

Originally proposed Sept. 25, 1789. Ratified May 7, 1992.

No law, varying the compensation for the services of the Senators and Representatives, shall take effect, until an election of Representatives shall have intervened

States' Rights Under the U.S. Constitution

Selective incorporation under the 14th Amendment

The U.S. Constitution has Articles and Amendments that established constitutional rights.

The provisions in the Bill of Rights (i.e., the first ten Amendments to the Constitution) were initially binding upon only the federal government.

In time, most of these provisions became binding upon the states through *selective incorporation* into the *due process clause* of the 14th Amendment (i.e., reverse incorporation).

When a provision is made binding on a state, a state can no longer restrict the rights guaranteed in that provision.

The 1st Amendment guarantees the freedoms of speech, press, religion, and assembly.

The 5th Amendment protects the right to grand jury proceedings in federal criminal cases.

The 6th Amendment guarantees a right to confront witnesses (i.e., Confrontation Clause).

The right to confront witnesses was not *selectively incorporated* into the due process clause of the 14th Amendment and is not binding upon the states.

Therefore, persons involved in state criminal proceedings as a defendant have no federal constitutional right to grand jury proceedings.

Whether an individual has a right to a grand jury becomes a question of state law.

The 10th Amendment, which is part of the Bill of Rights, was ratified on December 15, 1791. It states the Constitution's principle of federalism by providing that powers not granted to the federal government by the Constitution, nor prohibited to the States, are reserved to the States or the people.

Federalism in the United States

Federalism in the United States is the evolving relationship between state governments and the federal government.

The American government has evolved from a system of dual federalism to associative federalism.

In "Federalist No. 46," James Madison wrote that the states and national government "are in fact but different agents and trustees of the people, constituted with different powers."

Alexander Hamilton, in "Federalist No. 28," suggested that both levels of government would exercise authority to the citizens' benefit: "If their [the peoples'] rights are invaded by either, they can make use of the other as the instrument of redress."[3]

Because the states were preexisting political entities, the U.S. Constitution did not need to define or explain federalism in one section, but it often mentions the rights and responsibilities of state governments and state officials in relation to the federal government.

The federal government has certain *express powers* (also called *enumerated powers*), which are powers spelled out in the Constitution, including the right to levy taxes, declare war, and regulate interstate and foreign commerce.

Also, the *Necessary and Proper Clause* gives the federal government the *implied power* to pass any law "necessary and proper" to execute its express powers.

Enumerated powers of the Federal Government are contained in Article I, Section 8 of the U.S. Constitution.

Other powers—the *reserved powers*—are reserved to the people or the states under the 10th Amendment. The Supreme Court decision significantly expanded the power delegated to the federal government in *McCulloch v. Maryland* (1819) and the 13th, 14th and 15th, Amendments to the Constitution following the Civil War.

Law Essentials series

Constitutional Law	Criminal Law and Criminal Procedure
Contracts	Business Associations
Evidence	Conflict of Laws
Real Property	Family Law
Torts	Secured Transactions
Civil Procedure	Trusts and Estates

Visit our Amazon store

Comprehensive Glossary of Legal Terms

Over 2,100 essential legal terms defined and explained. An excellent reference source for law students, practitioners and readers seeking an understanding of legal vocabulary and its application.

Landmark U.S. Supreme Court Cases: Essential Summaries

Learn important constitutional cases that shaped American law. Understand how the evolving needs of society intersect with the U.S. Constitution. Short summaries of seminal Supreme Court cases focused on issues and holdings.

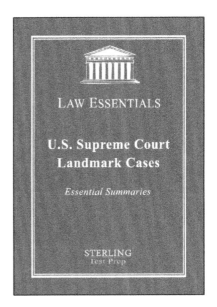

Visit our Amazon store

Frank J. Addivinola, Ph.D., J.D., L.LM., MBA

The lead author and chief editor of this preparation guide is Dr. Frank Addivinola. With his outstanding education, professional training, legal and business experience, and university teaching, Dr. Addivinola lent his expertise to develop this book.

Attorney Frank Addivinola is admitted to practice law in several jurisdictions. He has served as an academic advisor and mentor for students and practitioners.

Dr. Addivinola holds an undergraduate degree from Williams College. He completed his Masters at Harvard University, Masters in Biotechnology at Johns Hopkins University, Masters in Technology Management and MBA at the University of Maryland University College, J.D. and L.LM. from Suffolk University, and Ph.D. in Law and Public Policy from Northeastern University.

During his extensive teaching career, Dr. Addivinola taught university courses in Introduction to Law and developed law coursebooks. He received several awards for community service, research, and presentations.

Made in the USA
Monee, IL
26 April 2024

57546096R00105